Andrew

by William Garrott Brown

CONTENTS

I. THE WAXHAWS AND THE WILDERNESS

II. CONGRESS: THE BENCH: THE MILITIA

III. TOHOPEKA AND PENSACOLA

IV. NEW ORLEANS

V. THE SEMINOLES AND THE POLITICIANS

VI. THE WHITE HOUSE

ANDREW JACKSON

I

THE WAXHAWS AND THE WILDERNESS

In Lafayette Square, which fronts the White House at Washington, there is an equestrian statue of a very thin, long-headed old man whose most striking physical characteristics are the firm chin and lips and the bristling, upright hair. The piece is not a great work of art, but it gives one a strong impression of determination, if not of pugnacity. Sculptors have not the means to represent the human eye, else this impression might have been made stronger; for the old gentleman whose warlike aspect is here reproduced had a glance like a hawk's. He had, moreover, a habit of gazing fixedly at any one who attracted his attention. When he was angry, as he was quite frequently, few men could meet his look with composure. When he was in good humor, however, as he usually was when he dealt with his friends, or with women or children, his eyes could be very kindly, and his grim lips could part in a smile that was extremely attractive.

Not far away is the Treasury building. Were the horseman alive, by merely turning his head he could see its outline through the trees. There is a tradition in Washington that when this old man lived in the White House, and Congress voted to erect a new Treasury building, the old one being burned, there was some question of the exact spot on which it should stand. The question was put to him when he happened to be walking near the western end of Pennsylvania Avenue. He struck his cane on the ground and said shortly, "Put it here, sir,"--and there it stands. Whether or not the story is true, it is characteristic of the man and in keeping with the history of his times; for when Andrew Jackson was President most things were done at Washington just as he ordered them to be done. His friends declared that this was so because in most things his will stood for the will of the American people; his enemies, that they were done for no good reason whatever, but only because a despot commanded his slaves to do them.

To this day there is the same division of opinion. The historians still fight the same battle over him and his doings which in former times was fought out by famous orators in Congress, by the whole people at the polls. It is doubtful, indeed, if there ever will be, until the end of the Republic itself, an end of the dispute over the place which that slender figure with the bristling hair ought to have in American history. Had Andrew Jackson any good claim to statues and monuments, to the first place in the Republic, to popularity such as no other man had enjoyed since Washington, to power such as Washington himself had never exercised? Did he prove himself worthy of the place and power he held? To answer either yes or no with assurance one must patiently examine more books than Andrew Jackson ever glanced through in his whole life. This little book would hardly contain the full titles of them all. Yet it may perhaps be large enough to let the reader see what manner of man he was concerning whom so many bitter controversies have raged. Perhaps it may serve to explain how a Scotch-Irish boy, born to the deepest obscurity and the wretchedest poverty, and blessed, apparently, with no remarkable gifts of mind or body, came to have statues carved in his honor, towns and counties and cities named for him, long books written about him, a great party organized to do his bidding, the whole country time and again divided into those who were for him and those who were against him.

* * * * *

It is quite important, as Mr. Parton, the most painstaking of all his biographers, often observes, that this particular poor boy was of Scotch-Irish stock. That stock is again and again conspicuous in American history, and Andrew Jackson was in many respects the most thoroughly representative Scotch-Irishman of all the notable Americans who can trace their descent to the North of Ireland. Indeed, it may be said that he narrowly escaped being born in the North of Ireland, for his parents were living at Carrickfergus until two years before his birth. They landed in America in 1765, and made their home in a Scotch-Irish settlement, the Waxhaws, on the boundary line between the two Carolinas. Andrew Jackson, the father, and Elizabeth

Hutchinson, the mother, were married and had two sons before they left Carrickfergus. They were poor, and doubtless came to America for no other reason than to better their fortunes. They were still very poor when, in the early spring of the year 1767, the husband died. A few days later, March 15, a son was born to the widowed Elizabeth, and she named him Andrew. He himself in after years said that his birthplace was to the south of the state line, and called South Carolina his native State; but Mr. Parton's industrious researches make it seem more probable that the small log-house in which he was born was north of the line, in Union County, North Carolina.

The question is of less importance than the fact, of which there is no question, that he was born to the humblest circumstances in a new settlement of a new country, and that his childhood and boyhood were passed among people of little culture, whose lives were hard and bare. The boy got little education, and never was a scholar. To the day of his death, he wrote the English language with difficulty, making many errors of grammar and spelling, and spoke it with many peculiarities of pronunciation. Of other languages he knew nothing; of the great body of science, literature, and the arts he knew next to nothing. In fact, he probably got less from books than any other famous man in American history.

Little is authentically known of his early years. It is clear, however, that he was a mischievous, high-spirited boy, and often got into trouble. At least one anecdote is thoroughly in keeping with his career in manhood. Some of his playmates, so the story goes, once loaded a gun to the muzzle and gave it him to fire. As they expected, it kicked him over, but they missed the fun they looked for. He sprang to his feet white with rage, and exclaimed, with an oath, "If one of you laughs, I'll kill him!"--and no one laughed. The oath itself is not an unimportant part of the story, for it may as well be said at once that Andrew Jackson, until near the end of his life, had many such vices as swearing. He not only swore, but he frequently quarrelled and fought; he was at one time given to betting, particularly on horses; he drank, and he used tobacco constantly. All of these habits were common in the society to which he was born, and he did not escape them. But some things he did escape. He hated debt all his life, and was willing to do almost anything rather than incur it. He had the greatest reverence for women, and bore himself towards them with a courtesy and tenderness, a knightly purity of thought and word and deed, which the finest gentleman of the most ancient society in the world could not have surpassed.

When this pleasing fact is stated, one's thoughts turn naturally to his widowed mother, as to the most natural source of such an excellence in the son. All we know of her does indeed indicate that her influence on him was both strong and good: but we know very little. She was a simple, uncultivated person, like most of her neighbors, but her conduct during the harrowing scenes of the revolutionary war makes us think she was in some respects extraordinary. The struggle was nowhere rougher and fiercer than it was in the Carolinas. The notorious Colonel Tarleton operated in the Waxhaws neighborhood, and many dreadful stories of suffering and cruelty belong to that country and that time. The Jackson family had their full share of the fighting and the suffering. The two older boys, Hugh and Robert, enlisted. Young "Andy" himself, when he was barely in his teens, carried a musket. He and Robert were captured, and were released through the efforts of their mother, who brought about an exchange of prisoners. Soon afterwards, she went on a long and heroic journey to Charleston to nurse the sick Americans confined on the British prison ships there; and there she fell ill of the ship fever and died. Hugh and Robert both died in the service.

Andrew was thus left an orphan, weakened in body by the smallpox, which he took while he was in prison. Moreover, he bore on his head the mark of a blow from the sword of a British officer whose boots he had refused to polish. No man ever lived who had a simpler human way of loving those who befriended him and of hating those who hurt him than Andrew Jackson; and surely few men ever had better excuse than he for hating the British uniform. His feeling against the British was one of the things that colored his opinions on public questions; the supreme hour of his life was the hour when, at New Orleans, he had his revenge--full measure, heaped up, and running over--for all that he had suffered in the Waxhaws. Scholarly historians, passing rapidly over the events of his childhood, give many pages of learned criticism to the course he took on great public questions in later years, and gravely deplore the terrible passions that swayed him when, no doubt, he should have been as deliberate and calm as they are while they review his stormy life. But for those who would rather understand than judge him it surely cannot seem a small thing that he started out in life with such a heritage of bitter memories, such a schooling in hatred, as few children were ever cursed with. Passion and revenge are wrong, of course, but the sandy-haired, pockmarked lad of the Waxhaws had better excuse than most boys for failing to learn that lesson. It is doubtful, indeed, if any one ever took the trouble to teach it him. One little thing that stuck in his mind probably hurt worse than the sabre cut on his head. He did not even know where his mother's grave was.

It does not appear that during the next seven years, while he was growing to manhood, he gave himself with much industry either to study or to work. For six months he was employed in the shop of a saddler, but he seems to have learned more about filling saddles than about making them, for he became somewhat famous as a horseman even in a country where the love of horseflesh was universal. He got acquainted with some wealthy people from Charleston who were exiled until the British evacuated their city, and lived with them a sporting life which was beyond his means. After the peace he made a visit to Charleston, got into debt, got out of it by winning a wager, and grew somewhat graver in consequence of his experience. There is even some reason to believe that he went to work as a schoolmaster; and doubtless some backwoods schools of that period had masters as ignorant as Andrew Jackson. Finally, he resolved to study law, and in the winter of 1784-5 started out to find an office in which he might prepare himself for his profession. He found a place in the office of Mr. Spruce McCay, of Salisbury, North Carolina, an old-fashioned Southern town, where he made his home until 1788, when he was admitted to the bar.

All that is known of his life at Salisbury accords with what is known of his life at the Waxhaws. He was ready for a frolic or a fight at any hour of the day or night; he excelled in such sports as required swiftness and nerve; he was fond of practical jokes; he was not over fond of study, and never acquired any great knowledge of the law. At twenty, when his studies were finished, he is described as a tall, slender young fellow, with a thin, fair face and deep blue eyes, by no means handsome, but distinguished by considerable grace and dignity of manner; an exquisite rider and a capital shot; of an extraordinarily passionate temper, yet singularly swift, even when his anger was at white heat, to seize upon the right means to protect himself or discomfit an adversary; already somewhat of a leader, not by any eminence of talent or knowledge, but because he had a gift of leadership and was always intensely minded to have his way. The year of his admission to the bar, after a brief stay at Martinsville, a small North Carolina town, he got himself appointed solicitor, or public prosecutor, of the western district of Tennessee, and soon set out for the West.

The appointment of so young a man to such an office seems remarkable until one knows what Tennessee was like at that time, and what duties a solicitor was expected to discharge. The term Tennessee is, in fact, misleading. The region to which Jackson went still belonged to North Carolina, though its inhabitants had but a little while before made an attempt to set up a separate State under the name of Franklin. But of those who made the attempt the great majority had lived in that part of North Carolina's western lands which is now East Tennessee--a mountainous region of which Jonesboro, a squatter town of fifty or sixty log-houses, was the metropolis. Nashville, whither Jackson was bound, was nearly two hundred miles west of Jonesboro, and the Nashville settlement was as yet less than ten years old. It was founded in 1779 by Captain James Robertson with a little company of nine. The next year Colonel John Donelson, with a much larger party, including women and children, came from Virginia to join his friend Robertson. His journey was one of the most striking incidents in the peopling of the West, for it was made in flatboats which passed down the Holston into the Tennessee, down the Tennessee into the Ohio, up the Ohio into the Cumberland, and up the Cumberland to Nashville. It took four months to cover the two thousand miles or more, and there were bloody fights with Indians, sickness, and death by the way. When, eight years later, after an overland journey through a wilderness still almost unbroken and still infested with Indians, Jackson came to Nashville, he found Mrs. Donelson a widow, for her husband had been murdered; and he soon became an inmate of her home.

It was well for a widow in that wild country if she could procure men "boarders," even though she might not need to "take boarders" for a living; for every household needed men to protect it from the Indians. Immigration was increasing constantly, but the white population was still far too small to be safe. Within seven miles of Nashville, during the years 1780-1794, the Indians killed, on an average, one white person every ten days.

Life in such a country was even rougher and barer than in the Waxhaws. The houses were chiefly cabins made of unhewn logs, and the things which in older communities make the inside of houses attractive were almost wholly wanting. Such merchandise as was offered to the settlers had to be fetched hundreds of miles,--usually from Philadelphia,--and grew very dear by the time it reached them. For food, clothing, and shelter each family relied mainly on the handiwork of its own members. As in all frontier regions, the population was chiefly male. The brave women who took their share of the common work and hardship were treated with much respect, and did their part well, no doubt, but they had little leisure for those arts which brighten the lives and refine the characters of husbands and children.

Manners suited conditions. These builders of the West had more strength than gentleness, more shrewdness than wisdom, more courage than culture. They were the rough front which American civilization presented to the wilderness and the savage,--brave, hard-handed, themselves somewhat affected with the barbarism they came to displace, yet in all essentials of character true representatives of their masterful race. They were mainly of English or Scotch-Irish stock; and no other breeds of white men have ever shown such capacity as these two for dealing with inferior races and new countries. Their virtues were courage, energy, alertness, inventiveness, generosity, honesty, truth-speaking; their commonest faults were violence, combativeness, lax ways in business, intemperance, narrowness of mind.

They hated foreigners and Indians, and were ready to fight any one who behaved like an enemy or a critic; they held in honor women, their country, and brave men. Shut off from the greater world to the eastward, and having few pleasures such as most Americans may now enjoy, they filled their leisure hours with such sports as hunting, horse-racing, drinking bouts, fights, and lawsuits. The law, indeed, they held in great reverence; that race mark they had in common with all other societies made up of Englishmen and Americans of English descent. But they were even fonder of fighting than of the law, and the particular laws which were at once hardest to enforce and most in need of enforcement were those very simple laws which set forth the principle that private wrongs must be righted in the courts, which stand for the peace of the State, and not by the "wild justice" of revenge.

The difficult and dangerous work of keeping order and of enforcing business obligations fell largely to the "solicitor;" and one need not wonder that there was no great scramble for the office, so that a very young man, with no experience at the bar and little knowledge of law, got the appointment. His duties were simple enough, but he had no reason to complain of being left in idleness. The court records of the period show a picturesque assortment of assaults, street-fights, pistollings, gougings, and the like. Men who took such methods to adjust their differences were not apt to show any great respect to a prosecutor aged twenty-one. The majesty of the law had need of a vigorous rather than a learned representative; and the representative had need of other weapons than those supplied by the law books if he meant to make his authority respected and yet keep a whole skin on his body. If he proved weak and timid, he was sure to be despised; if determined and relentless, he was sure to make enemies; if incautious and unwary, he would probably get himself shot. It is doubtful, however, if any better man than young Jackson could have been found for the place, and that is almost the same thing as saying that no better place could have been found for him. To the office and his new surroundings he brought the qualities they supremely demanded,--a will that no man ever subdued, a desperate courage which not even the Tennesseans could match, and a swift, intuitive perception of the way to act in emergencies.

According to all accounts, he was successful from the first in his trying work, and his success in that brought him other work as a lawyer and a rapid rise to prominence in the community. He became well acquainted, for his work required much travelling about. He learned the country itself. On his long journeys he was frequently in danger from the Indians, and learned their ways and how to cope with them. Sometimes he slept alone in the woods, or even lay all night awake, his hand on his rifle. Once his readiness and nerve alone saved himself and a party of travellers from surprise and massacre. Whether he dealt with Indians who beset his pathway through the wilderness, or white men who would not let the law take its course, it is not on record that he ever turned aside from his purpose. In ten years he was the possessor of a considerable estate, chiefly in land. And he had not accumulated property by neglecting his duties as solicitor. When certain intruders on Indian lands were giving trouble, Governor Blount said: "Let the district attorney, Mr. Jackson, be informed. He will be certain to do his duty, and the offenders will be punished."

But the district attorney did not escape the consequences of his firmness and courage. He had so many "difficulties" that even in that country he soon got a reputation for readiness to fight. A mass of anecdote and tradition about his early quarrels has come down to us. Some of these affairs seem to have been undignified and rather ludicrous scuffles: in one of them Jackson overcame a huge antagonist by poking him with the point--or, as Jackson himself pronounced it, the "pint"--of a fence rail. Other quarrels followed the dignified procedure of the duello. They were all subject to the condemnation which our gentler civilization pronounces on violence as a means of ending disputes, but no doubt they helped the young lawyer into the prominence he had won by the time Tennessee was ready to become a State.

The most important event of this early period of Jackson's life was his marriage. It was first solemnized early in 1791, and a second time in January, 1794. The second ceremony was due to the painful discovery that at the time of the first his wife was not fully released from a former marriage. She was

Rachel, daughter of John Donelson, the pioneer, and when Jackson first came to Tennessee she was already married to one Lewis Robards. Robards was a jealous husband. He made charges against his wife concerning several men, and finally concerning Jackson, although the facts that have come down to us and the opinions of those who knew most about the affair all go to show that Jackson acted as a chivalrous protector of a distressed woman, and never knowingly committed any offence against his accuser's home. Robards and Rachel Donelson had been married in Kentucky, then a part of Virginia, and Virginia had no law of divorce. In 1790 the Virginia legislature, acting on a petition of Robards, authorized the supreme court of Kentucky to try the case and grant him a divorce if it should find his charges against his wife and Jackson to be true. Somehow, Jackson and Mrs. Robards were persuaded that this act of the Virginia legislature was itself a divorce, and so they were married. In 1793, however, Robards brought suit before the Kentucky court, and the court, finding on the facts as they then existed, when the accused couple were living together as man and wife, granted the decree. In order, therefore, to make sure of a legal marriage, Jackson had the ceremony repeated.

It was a most unfortunate situation for an honest man and an honest woman, and saddened a union which was otherwise pure and beautiful; for to the day of her death Jackson and his wife loved each other most tenderly. It brought into his life a new element of bitterness and passion. Whoever, by the slightest hint, referred to the irregularity of his marriage, became his mortal enemy. For such he kept his pistols always ready, and more than one incautious man found to his cost what it meant to breathe a word on that forbidden subject. One such man was no less a person than John Sevier, "the Commonwealth Builder," who struck such a good blow for American independence at the battle of King's Mountain in the revolutionary war, and who was Governor of Tennessee when the trouble with Jackson occurred.

The painful facts of his marriage, and the criticism of his wife, had another effect on Jackson which in time became important to the whole country. Through that experience his chivalrous feeling for women was developed into a quixotic readiness to be the champion of any woman whom he found distressed or slandered.

II

CONGRESS: THE BENCH: THE MILITIA

In 1796 Jackson took his seat as a member of the convention called to frame a constitution for the State of Tennessee. He thus entered on a brief career of public service, in the course of which he held three important offices. In the autumn of 1796 he was chosen to be Tennessee's first representative in Congress. A year later he was appointed United States Senator, and held the office until he resigned in April, 1798. From 1798 until 1804, he was a justice of the Supreme Court of Tennessee.

These were all high places for so young a man, and one naturally expects his biographer to linger for many pages over his course while he held them. The fact that he held them is indeed important, for it shows how strongly he had established himself in Tennessee. But very little need be said of what he did while he held them. Indeed, it is amazing how little can be said.

In the convention he served on the committee to draft the constitution and took a somewhat prominent part in the debates, and there is also a tradition that he suggested the name of the State; but no notable feature of the constitution is clearly due to him. It might, however, have been due to the presence in the convention of such fiery spirits as he that it adopted a rule of order which throws into comical prominence the warlike character of early Tennesseans. Rule 8 declared: "He that digresseth from the subject to fall on the person of any member shall be suppressed by the Speaker."

The scant record of Jackson's services in the House of Representatives and in the Senate is of little importance to us save in three respects. It throws some light on his political opinions at that period; it gives us a glimpse of him as he appeared against the background of the most elegant society then existing in

America, for Congress was sitting in Philadelphia, which had sixty-five thousand inhabitants; and it led to one or two friendships which had an important bearing on his later career.

His opinions, however, were not expressed in speeches. He addressed the House but twice, both times on a resolution for paying troops whom General Sevier had led against the Indians without any order from the national government. The resolution passed, and added to Jackson's popularity at home. In the Senate it is not on record that he ever spoke at all. Many years afterwards, Thomas Jefferson, who was Vice-President in 1797-8, gave to Daniel Webster a rather curious explanation of the Tennessee Senator's silence. The accuracy of Webster's report of his famous interview with Jefferson at Monticello in 1824 has been questioned, but if it is correct, this is what Jefferson said of Jackson: "His passions are terrible. When I was president of the Senate, he was Senator, and he could never speak on account of the rashness of his feelings. I have seen him attempt it repeatedly, and as often choke with rage."

His votes, however, and a few letters show clearly enough where he stood on the questions of the day. Parties were hardly yet formed under the Constitution, but in the strife between the followers of Hamilton, who went for a strong national government, and who became the Federalist party, on the one hand, and, on the other hand, the followers of Jefferson, who went for the rights of the States and distrusted a strong national government, and who became the Republican party, he sided with Jefferson. Indeed, he belonged to the extreme faction of the Republicans, to which the term "Democrats" was applied, at first as a reproach. He favored the French, who were at war with England, and opposed the treaty with England which John Jay had just negotiated. He even went so far as to vote, with eleven others, against the address presented to President Washington after his final speech to Congress. The address was mainly given over to thanks for Washington's great services to his country and to praise of his administration. The handful that opposed it showed at least courage. One of them, Edward Livingston, of New York, afterwards defended himself by drawing a distinction between

Washington and his administration. At that time the partisans of France were very bitter over the firm course Washington took to keep the country out of the European contest, and over the treaty with England.

Livingston was one of the men with whom Jackson at this time formed a lasting friendship. He was an accomplished gentleman, a very able lawyer, and an advanced Republican. Another was William Duane, Jefferson's friend, the editor of "The Aurora," a newspaper which helped to build up the Republican party. A third was Aaron Burr, who then stood very high among the Republican leaders, and who excelled all other public men in charm of manner.

Another leading Republican of the time, Albert Gallatin, recalled Jackson afterwards as "a tall, lank, uncouth-looking personage, with long locks of hair hanging over his face, and a cue down his back tied in an eel-skin; his dress singular, his manners and deportment that of a rough backwoodsman." Taking this with Jefferson's description of him, it seems clear that he made no strong impression at Philadelphia, and found himself out of place in the national legislature. Who, then, would have dreamed that the accomplished Livingston should win his highest fame by preparing a state paper for this unlettered person's signature; that this rough backwoodsman should alone of all Americans surpass the polished Burr in the charm of his manners; that Duane's little son should one day be called by his father's unpromising acquaintance to a place such as even Jefferson's friendship never conferred upon Duane himself. Of all who knew Jackson in Washington, Burr seems to have had the strongest hopes for his future.

Scant as are the traces of his labors as a legislator, even scanter are the records of his career on the bench during the six years that followed. The reports of the decisions of the Tennessee Supreme Court in this period are extremely meagre; not one decision is preserved as Jackson's. But the stories told of Judge Jackson, like the stories told of the solicitor, the general, the president, are legion. One must suffice. A gigantic blacksmith named Bean had committed a crime and the sheriff dared not arrest him. "Summon me," said the judge, and himself walked down from the bench, found the criminal, and arrested him. It was while he was judge that his quarrel with John Sevier, who was again governor in 1803, came finally to a head. Two years before, the two men had been rivals for the office of major-general in the militia, and by a single vote Jackson had won, so that he was both general and judge when he and the governor met in what seemed likely to prove a fatal combat. However, neither was killed, and the quarrel was patched up. In 1804 Judge Jackson resigned. He had not yet found his true place in the public service. But he kept his commission in the militia, and those who like to magnify the work of chance may argue that the single vote by which he got that office determined his career.

But he had years to live before it was made plain to him what his career should be; and during those years, from 1804 to 1813, his energies were given chiefly to planting and business. His affairs had become somewhat involved while he was a judge, and to restore his fortunes he entered into trade and set up a store. In this and other enterprises a stalwart Tennessean named John Coffee was his partner, and between the two there grew a bond of friendship which lasted until death broke it. Jackson had considerable shrewdness in trade, and his reputation for paying his debts promptly was of great value, but he had more success in planting and stock-raising than in any other money-making enterprise. His judgment of horses was exceptionally good. From his famous stallion, Truxton, a great racer in his day, many Tennessee thoroughbreds of the present time are descended. Horse-racing was Jackson's favorite sport, and was a source of profit also. In 1805 he first occupied the estate which became so well known as "The Hermitage," where he built a block-house of three rooms; the mansion so often displayed in pictures was not built until 1819. In the log-house, however, no less than in the mansion which was to follow, he offered to guests of high and low degree a hospitality which would have been extraordinary outside of the Southern States. Probably his planter life had some effect on his manners, and helped him to acquire that mingling of cordiality and distinction which in those days gave a peculiar charm to the gentlemen of the South.

Even in his quarrels, violent, passionate, and wilful as he was, he usually bore himself in a way to make a deep impression on the impressionable people among whom he lived. Unfortunately, his quarrels did not grow fewer as he grew older, for he never learned the difference between mere opposition to his will, which might be conscientious and honest, and personal enmity to himself. Like most men of that region and time, he carried his personal feelings, his likes and dislikes, into all the affairs of life. In 1803-4, when he wished to be governor of Orleans Territory, the Tennessee congressmen urged President Jefferson to appoint him, but he was represented to the President as "a man of violent passions, arbitrary in his disposition, and frequently engaged in broils and disputes."

The most celebrated and perhaps the worst of all his quarrels was that with Charles Dickinson, a young man of prominence, a duellist, and a marvellous shot. It was a long quarrel, beginning, apparently, over a projected race between Truxton and Plow Bay, a horse in which Dickinson was interested. Other persons were involved before the quarrel ended. General Jackson publicly caned one Thomas Swann who had contrived to get himself mixed up in the affair. Coffee, acting as Jackson's friend, had a duel with one McNairy, and was severely wounded. Finally, for no sufficient cause which the printed accounts discover, Jackson and Dickinson met in Kentucky, each bent on killing his man. The word being given, Dickinson fired quickly, and with perfect aim; a puff of dust flew up from the breast of Jackson's coat. But he kept his feet, drew his left arm across his breast, slowly raised his pistol, and pulled the trigger. The hammer stopped at the half-cock. He cocked it again, aimed deliberately, fired, and killed his man. His own life he owed to the thinness of his body, for Dickinson had hit the spot where he thought his adversary's heart was beating. Jackson had purposely allowed the other to fire first, expecting to be hit, and fearing that if he, too, fired hurriedly, the shock would spoil his aim. "I should have hit him," he said afterwards, "had he shot me through the brain." It is supposed that his hatred of Dickinson was really due, not to the confused dispute over the race, but to something Dickinson had said in his cups about Mrs. Jackson. Whatever the provocation, the bloody story is revolting enough; but the picture of Jackson's grim, erect figure, his hawklike eyes terrible with hatred, the ball in his breast, the pistol in his hand, must take its place alongside those other pictures and statues of him which all Americans know.

But if Jackson was a terrible enemy, he was also the most faithful of friends. Many men feared and hated him; many also loved him, and he himself would go as far to help a friend as to crush an enemy. One of his friends was a certain Patten Anderson, who seems always to have been getting into trouble, but whom the general never deserted. Once Anderson got into a fight at one end of a long table where a public dinner was being served, and was in great danger until Jackson, who sat at the other end, noticed the scuffle. "I'm coming, Patten," he cried, and promptly leaped on the table and strode through dinner to the rescue. Anderson was killed at last, and Jackson was a witness at the trial of his slayer. He was asked if the unfortunate Anderson was not given in his lifetime to quarrelling. "Sir," said Jackson, "my friend, Patten Anderson, was a natural enemy to scoundrels."

His friendship for Aaron Burr came very near involving him in serious difficulties. In 1805, when Burr was on his first visit to the Southwest, he went to Nashville, and was entertained most cordially at The Hermitage. He was there again on his return, and made with his host a contract for boats and supplies to be used in that mysterious enterprise which has so puzzled American historians. Burr declared he had no designs hostile to the United States, and Jackson believed him. When, a year later, the whole country was in a sort of panic over Burr's suspected treason, Jackson offered to President Jefferson the services of the militia under his command, and promptly took measures to thwart any treasonable movement that might be afoot in the West; but he was soon convinced that Burr was suspected unjustly, and never for a moment deserted him in his trouble. He went to Richmond to testify at his trial, and while there made a public speech full of bitterness against those who, as he thought, were persecuting his friend. He himself was at first strongly suspected of complicity in Burr's project, but there is absolutely no reason to believe that Andrew Jackson ever in his life looked upon an enemy of his country otherwise than as his own mortal foe. His faults were many, but he loved his country simply, and with all his heart.

It seems clear, however, that Jackson, and in fact the whole Southwest, sympathized very strongly with the design which many in that quarter at first thought Burr to entertain; the design, namely, of seizing West Florida or Texas, or perhaps both. The United States were at that time, as they were before and after, very close to war with Spain. Spain still had possession of the Floridas, although the United States claimed that West Florida, extending along the Gulf coast from the Perdido River to the "Island of New Orleans," was included in the Louisiana purchase. To drive the Spaniards out of West Florida was an ardent desire of Jackson's. Ten years before, when the Eastern States had shown little interest in the development of the Southwest, and had seemed to prefer commercial privileges with the Spanish colonies to the free navigation of the Mississippi, which the Western country needed for its development, Spanish agents had endeavored to stir up disaffection in the Southwest, looking to the separation of that region from the Union. At that time, many people in the East, knowing little of the Westerners, had suspected them of lending an ear to Spain's tempting whispers. That was one reason why such a panic arose over Burr, for he had always been a champion of the Southwest, and the pioneers liked him. After the failure and disgrace of Burr the stage was cleared for another leader in the southwestward movement. And who so likely to take the role as the patriotic and warlike general of the Tennessee militia?

Jackson had a chance to play that role in a small way when Silas Dinsmore, the United States agent among the Choctaws, whose lands lay in Mississippi Territory, refused to allow persons to pass through the Choctaw country with negroes unless they showed passports for the negroes. Dinsmore had a law of Congress behind him, but a treaty between the United States and the Choctaws provided for a road through the Choctaw country which should be "a highway for citizens of the United States and the Choctaws." Jackson, passing along the road with some slaves, dared the agent to interfere. He also exerted himself to bring about the removal of Dinsmore, and, as his wont was, made a personal matter of the dispute. His feeling was so strong that years afterwards, when Dinsmore, happening to meet him, made a courteous advance, the general sternly repelled it.

The quarrel with Dinsmore occurred in 1812. Andrew Jackson was then forty-five years old. He was well known in Tennessee as a successful planter, a breeder and racer of horses, a swearer of mighty oaths, a faithful and generous man to his friends, a chivalrous man to women, a hospitable man at his home, a desperate and relentless man in personal conflicts, a man who always did the thing he set himself to do. But as yet he had never found anything to do that was important enough to bring him before the country at large. Outside of Tennessee, few men had ever heard his name. At Washington he was probably distrusted, so far as he was known at all, because of his championship of Burr and his quarrel with Dinsmore, and because he had been for Monroe instead of Madison for President. He was ardently in favor of war with Great Britain because of the impressment of American seamen and other grievances which the United States had borne for years, but there seemed to be little likelihood of his getting a chance to play a part in the war if it should come. The war was declared in June, 1812. A member of Congress, on his way home after voting for the declaration, had a talk with Aaron Burr, who was now living in retirement in New York. "I know," said Burr, "that my word is not worth much with Madison; but you may tell him from me that there is an unknown man in the West, named Andrew Jackson, who will do credit to a commission in the army."

It is said, indeed, that Jackson was twice recommended to President Madison for a commission in the regular army, and twice rejected. Many years later, Thomas H. Benton told in Congress how he himself, who was in 1812 a young lawyer in Nashville and a militia officer under Jackson, found in his mail one morning an act of Congress authorizing the President to accept organized bodies of volunteers. It was a raw day in February, but young Benton at once drew up a plan for offering Jackson's militia command to the government, rode to The Hermitage to find the general, "and came upon him," so Mr. Benton's story goes, "in the twilight, sitting alone before the fire, a lamb and a child between his knees. He started a little, called a servant to remove the two innocents to another room, and explained to me how it was. The child had cried because the lamb was out in the cold, and begged him to bring it in--which he had done to please the child, his adopted son." That is a far pleasanter picture than the other we saw just now of Jackson the duellist, but this also is a characteristic picture, and should go into the gallery; for Jackson, like many another man who has been denied children of his own, was singularly tender with little folk. It is certainly good to be able to think of him, fierce man that he was, as turning from fondling a child to enter on his soldier's career.

Mr. Benton's account of the matter is questioned, but it is certain that Jackson offered his services, with those of 2500 volunteers, immediately after the declaration of war. The government accepted the offer, but left him in idleness until October, 1812, when the governor of Tennessee was asked for volunteers, ostensibly to reinforce General Wilkinson at New Orleans. The governor in turn called upon General Jackson, and he, setting to work with the utmost enthusiasm, issued to the volunteers the first of those eminently Jacksonian addresses wherewith he was wont to hearten his followers. On January 7, 1813, the command set forth, the infantry by river, the cavalry, under John Coffee, by land. By the middle of February all were united at Natchez, Mississippi, where the expedition was halted to await further orders. Week after week passed by, and finally, late in March, to the general's rage and disgust, he heard from the Secretary of War that the causes of the expedition had ceased to exist, and that he was to consider his command "dismissed from the public service"--and not one word as to any provision for getting the men home!

Jackson's resolution was instantly taken and firmly carried out. He refused to disband the men at Natchez, and marched them home, pledging his own credit for the necessary expenses. His course commanded the approval of the State and won him the devotion of the men. It was the first of many occasions on which, while acting as a military officer, he dared to do the thing he thought to be right, no matter how irregular it was. On the journey home, his soldierly behavior in trying circumstances won him his famous nickname.

The men spoke of him as being "tough as hickory," and so came to call him "Hickory," and finally, with affection, "Old Hickory." Before he reached Nashville he again offered his command for service in Canada, but no reply came. In May, he dismissed it, and it seemed as if he were not going to have any soldier's career at all.

Benton, who had served in the expedition as an aid, went to Washington and with difficulty persuaded the War Department to pay the expenses of the march from Natchez. When he returned to Nashville, it was to find that in a duel between Jesse Benton, his brother, and one Carroll, the general had acted as Carroll's second. A bitter quarrel between Jackson and the Bentons followed; before it ended, Jackson swore "by the Eternal" he would horsewhip Thomas Benton on sight. They met at a Nashville hotel. Jesse Benton was there, and also John Coffee and Stokeley Hays, friends of Jackson's. There was a rough-and-tumble fight. Thomas Benton fell down a stairway; Jesse Benton was stabbed; Jackson was shot in the shoulder and severely wounded. He was put to bed in the old Nashville Inn, a famous hostelry of the time, and while he lay helpless from a wound so ignobly won, the call was on its way which should at last summon him to the work for which he was fittest. He was to pass from an action such as no biographer can defend to deeds which none can fail to praise. Jackson the duellist must give place to Jackson the soldier. Yet all fighting is akin, and it was but a change of scene and purpose that turned the man of the tavern brawl into the man of The Horseshoe and New Orleans; for it happened that there was nowhere in the Southwest, perhaps nowhere in the country, any other man quite so sure to have his way, whether in a street fight or in a battle.

III

TOHOPEKA AND PENSACOLA

The call that now came to Jackson was chiefly due to a very picturesque character of the times: the man who is said to have been the only rival of Burr and Jackson in the impression he made upon all beholders by his manner and bearing. The call came, indeed, from the southward, but probably it would never have come but for the work of Tecumseh (or Tecumthe), the famous Shawnee warrior and orator, whose home was in the Northwest. For years Tecumseh had been striving to unite the red men of the West and South in a supreme effort to roll back the swelling tide of white immigration. In 1811 he made a pilgrimage to the southern tribes, and his most fervent appeal was to that powerful body of Indians known as the Creek Confederacy, who lived in what is now the eastern part of Alabama and the southwestern part of Georgia. These proud and warlike Indians were divided into two branches. The Upper Creeks had their homes along the Coosa and Tallapoosa rivers, and their villages extended some distance down the Alabama, which is formed by the junction of those two streams. The Lower Creek towns were on both sides of the Chattahoochee, which now separates southern Georgia from southern Alabama. The so-called Confederacy, a loose sort of alliance, claimed for a hunting ground the lands extending westward to the watershed between the Alabama and Tombigbee rivers, which unite to form the Mobile. But in the fork of these two rivers and along the Mobile and the Tombigbee were growing settlements of white men. The growth of these settlements was watched with disfavor and suspicion by the Creeks. A strong party, the Red Sticks, or hostiles, listened readily to Tecumseh's teaching. When he left for his home in the distant Northwest many were already dancing the "war-dance of the Lakes."

The outbreak of the war with England came in good time for Tecumseh's plans. He at once put himself in alliance with the British, and in the summer of 1813 the Creek Red Sticks heard that they could get arms and ammunition at Pensacola, the capital of Spanish Florida. Spain was at peace with the United States, but Red Sticks were seen thronging to Pensacola and returning with arms and ammunition. The whites of the Mobile and Tombigbee country, then part of Mississippi Territory, organized for defence, waylaid a party returning from Pensacola, and were at first victorious, then defeated, in the so-called Battle of Burnt Corn. Thoroughly alarmed, the settlers now took refuge in stockades and forts. The military authorities of the United States made ready to defend Mobile, but recently seized from the Spaniards. At Fort Mims, near the point where the Alabama and Tombigbee form the Mobile, five hundred and fifty-three men, women, and children were pent up in an ill-planned inclosure, defended by a small force under an incompetent though courageous officer named Beasley. On the morning of August 30, 1813, Beasley was writing to his superior, General Claiborne, that he could hold the fort against any number of the enemy. At that very moment a thousand warriors lay hidden in a ravine but a few hundred yards from the open gate of the stockade. Their principal leader was William Weatherford, "the Red Eagle," a half-breed of much intelligence and dauntless courage. At noon, when the drums beat the garrison to dinner, the Indians rushed to the attack. At the end of the hot August day there remained of the fort but a smouldering heap of ruins, ghastly with human bodies. Only a handful of the inmates escaped to spread the horrible news among the terrified settlers. Swift runners set off eastward, westward, and northward for help. A shudder ran over the whole country. The Southwest turned from the remoter events of the war in Canada to the disaster at home. "The Creeks!" "Weatherford!" "Fort Mims!" were the words on everybody's lips, while the major-general of the Tennessee militia still lay helpless from his shameful wound.

From Mississippi on the west, from Georgia on the east, and from Tennessee on the north, volunteer armies were soon on the march for the Creek country. Tennessee, indeed, sent two different bodies of men. One came from East Tennessee, commanded by General John Cocke; the other came from West Tennessee, and at its head, pale and weak, his arm in a sling, his shoulder too sore to bear the weight of an epaulette, was Andrew Jackson. He had issued his orders from his bed. When a member of the legislature, come to discuss the expedition with him, expressed regret that he would not be able to lead it, the sick man muttered, with the inevitable oath, that he would lead it. But from the beginning to the end of his military service he was paying the penalty, not merely of the quarreling which had brought him wounds, but of intemperate eating and drinking, which had ruined his digestion. Sometimes he was tortured for hours with pains that could be relieved only by hanging his body, like a garment hung to dry, face downward, over the back of a chair, or, if he were on the march, over a sapling stripped and bent for the purpose.

By the second week in October, Jackson was at Huntsville, on the Tennessee River. The entire command numbered about 2700. Its supplies were to come by water from Knoxville, in East Tennessee, but the upper part of the river was not navigable by reason of the dryness of the season. Jackson stormed at the delay, but used the time in drilling his men and scouring the country with Coffee's cavalry. Then he cut his way over the mountains to a higher point on the river, hoping to find the supplies. His energy was great, but without food he could not, as he desired, dash at once into the enemy's country. He moved southward when he had food, halted when it gave out, and finally reached the Coosa. From his camp there, which he named Fort Strother, he dispatched Coffee to strike a first blow against the Creek town of Tallusahatchee. Coffee destroyed the town, and not a warrior escaped, for the whites were bitterly revengeful. A slain mother embracing a living infant was found among the dead. Jackson himself took care of the child, sent it to The Hermitage, and he and his wife reared it to manhood.

The next blow was struck at Talladega, thirty miles below Fort Strother, where a body of friendly Indians were besieged by a larger body of Red Sticks. Relying on General White, who was in the neighborhood with a force of Cocke's East Tennesseans, to protect Fort Strother, Jackson marched by night to Talladega. There, however, a dispatch reached him from White, who announced that he must return to Cocke. So at sunrise Jackson threw himself on the enemy, routed him with great loss, relieved the friendly Indians, and then marched back to camp, to find no provisions, and the sick and wounded as hungry as the rest. From that time the struggle with famine was for weeks his principal business. Ill as he was, he and his officers would have nothing the men could not have. A soldier coming to him to beg for food, he thrust his hand into his pocket, drew out some acorns, and courteously invited the man to share his dinner.

Jackson was disposed to blame General Cocke for the trouble about supplies, because Cocke had undertaken to obtain supplies in Knoxville for both commands; but it seems clear now that Cocke was not to blame. Soon after the battle of Talladega Jackson's feeling against Cocke was strengthened. The warriors of the Hillabee towns, a part of the Creek Confederacy, sent a messenger to Jackson to sue for peace. He gave them his terms, and the messenger was returning to the Hillabees when General White, of Cocke's command, ignorant of what was going on, marched upon a Hillabee town, killed many of the warriors, and captured the women and children. Jackson, grieved and enraged at a blunder which probably prolonged the war and certainly made it fiercer, was easily persuaded that Cocke, his inferior officer, was trying to win laurels for himself, and in the end his anger led him to do grave injustice to a man who appears to have been faithful and honorable.

And now for ten weeks the will of Andrew Jackson was tried to the uttermost. His starving troops were constantly on the verge of mutiny. The command was made up of two classes,--the militia, called into service against the Indians, and the volunteers, who had first enlisted for the expedition down the Mississippi. The militia, disheartened, started for Tennessee. Jackson drew up the volunteers across their pathway, and drove them back to camp. Then the volunteers, in their turn, prepared to move northward, and he stopped them with the militia. The mounted men were permitted to go to Huntsville to get food for their horses, and most of them went on to their homes. The infantry, sullen and distrustful, were kept in camp only by the promise that in two days supplies would come from Nashville, whither Jackson was sending letter after letter to stir up the authorities. At the end of two days nothing had come. A few brave men volunteered to defend the camp while with the rest the general marched northward in search of food. The supplies soon came in sight, and the men were fed; but now they refused to go back to camp, and again turned northward. Jackson, with Coffee and a handful of others, threw himself in front of them, and with blazing eyes and dreadful oaths cowed them into obedience. Again they threatened mutiny, and once more, alone, on horseback, a musket in his hand, his disabled arm in its sling, he faced them, and swore he would shoot the first man who stirred. They hesitated, wavered, yielded.

Seeing, however, that nothing could be done with the volunteers, Jackson finally permitted them to go, keeping with him the militia and a small body of Cocke's men. The militia claimed that their term would expire January 4, 1814; the term of Cocke's men would expire a week later. Anxiously awaiting reinforcements, Jackson got, instead, a letter from Governor Blount advising him to give up the struggle. But he would not give up; his magnificent spirit rose higher with every blow. He wrote the governor a letter that taught him his duty. Through the governor, in fact, that letter roused the whole State, and soon a new army was on the way from West Tennessee, while Cocke was marching another force southward from East Tennessee. With some five hundred raw recruits that reached him before Cocke's first command left, Jackson held Fort Strother. He even ventured to make a raid into the enemy's country, aiming at the town of Emuckfau. The Indians attacked him. He repulsed them, but soon made up his mind to return. On his way back, he was again attacked while crossing a creek, his rear guard was driven in, and for a moment a panic and rout was imminent. But the valor of a few men saved the army, and he got safely back to Fort Strother.

He did not move again until the middle of March, and then he had five thousand men. Cocke, for a speech addressed to his troops when they threatened mutiny, was sent to Nashville under arrest. To stamp out insubordination among the men from West Tennessee, a youth named Woods, who had been found guilty of mutiny, was shot before the whole army. The thirty-ninth regiment of regulars was now a part of the command, and the general proposed to use them, whenever occasion offered, to suppress insubordination among the volunteers. But from this time he had little of that to deal with, and was free to grapple with the Creeks, who had so far held their own against the Georgians and Mississippians.

The centre of their resistance was the Hickory Ground, near the fork of the Coosa and Tallapoosa; but the final blow was struck at a bend in the Tallapoosa midway between its source and mouth. The spot was called by the

Indians Tohopeka; by the whites, The Horseshoe. Across the neck of a small peninsula the hostiles had thrown up a rough line of breastworks. On the banks of the river they had gathered a number of canoes. Within the defences was a force of Red Sticks estimated at nine hundred, and several hundred women and children.

Jackson moved down the Coosa to a point nearly even with Tohopeka, established a new camp, and by the evening of March 28 he was in front of the enemy with about three thousand men, including a considerable body of friendly Indians. Resolving to make thorough work of it, he dispatched Coffee, with the friendly Indians and the cavalry, to surround the bend on the opposite bank. The next morning, with the artillery, he opened fire on the breastworks. Coffee, meantime, threw a force across the river and attacked the enemy from the rear. The line of breastworks was carried by assault. The slaughter of Creeks was dreadful. As usual, they fought to the last. Five hundred and fifty-seven bodies were found in the bend, and many perished trying to escape across the river. Jackson's loss was about two hundred killed and wounded.

Tohopeka broke down the organized resistance of the Indians. When Jackson, a few days later, turned southward, he was able to march on to the Hickory Ground without fighting another battle. The Red Sticks for the most part fled to their kindred, the Seminoles, in Florida; but some came in and submitted to the iron hand which had crushed them. Jackson had been at the Hickory Ground but a short time when Weatherford himself came in and surrendered. Some of the men, remembering Fort Mims, would have done violence to the fallen chief, but Jackson protected him. Soon afterwards, General Pinckney, of the regular army, arrived at Fort Jackson, which had been built in the river fork, and took command. When he ordered the Tennesseans to return to their homes, Jackson went with them, and his fellow citizens at Nashville gave him the first of many triumphal receptions. His eight months' work in the wilderness had made him easily the first man of Tennessee. Georgia had had a better chance than Tennessee to crush the Indians, for the distance and the natural obstacles were less; but Georgia had no such leader as Andrew Jackson. Another reward soon reached him. In May, General William Henry Harrison resigned his commission, and in his place Jackson was appointed major-general in the army of the United States. He was put in command of the southwestern district, including Mobile and New Orleans.

But on his way to his post he had to stop again at Fort Jackson and complete his work among the Creeks. Acting under orders from the government, he compelled the chiefs there assembled, practically all of whom had been friendly to the United States during the war, to sign an "agreement and capitulation" by which they ceded to the United States all the land which they had claimed to the west of the Coosa. He carried the matter through with a high hand, but the Creeks themselves admired him and put into the agreement a cession of land to himself. It was, of course, not permissible for a negotiator to accept such a gift from the other party. However, the land was part of the region claimed by the United States and surrendered by the Creeks, and as a matter of fact, Jackson never got possession of it. This "treaty," as it was improperly called, was signed August 9, 1814, and then Jackson was free to take up his new duties as the defender of the Southwest against the British.

Up to this time, except for the war with the Creeks and the bloodless capture of Mobile, the Southwest had taken little part in the contest. On land, the war had been mainly an affair of the North, where the Americans had been trying to wrest Canada from the mother country, and of the Northwest, where the British and the Indians had taken the offensive. The death of Tecumseh at the battle of the Thames, in November, 1813, had made an end of that combination, and General William Henry Harrison had won some honor by his management of the campaign. But the several attempts at invading Canada were neither successful nor glorious. On the whole, the land campaigns of the Americans had been utterly disappointing. The little American navy had indeed covered itself with glory, both on the high seas and on the Great Lakes; but from the seas, where it was vastly overmatched by Great Britain's immense naval resources, it had practically disappeared by the autumn of 1814. Only a few privateers still preyed on British commerce. And now, by the overthrow of Napoleon, Great Britain was left free to employ against America all those ships with which Nelson had won for her the empire of the sea, and those superb soldiers who, under Wellington, had driven the French out of Spain. Regiments of these veterans were sent to Canada. In August, an expedition under General Ross landed on the coast of Chesapeake Bay, defeated an American force at Bladensburg, took Washington, and burned the capitol and the President's mansion. The enemy was stronger than ever, and the United States were at the point of exhaustion.

Moreover, the ruling class in one important section of the country was rather inclined to weaken than to help the government. The Federalist leaders in New England were against the French, against President Madison, against the war. They had been in opposition ever since President Jefferson went into office in 1801. Distrusting the Southwest, and opposing the expansion of the country in that direction, they had talked about a breaking up of the Union when Louisiana was purchased in 1803, and again when the State of Louisiana was admitted in 1811-12. When the war began, the governors of several New England States refused to turn their militia over to the Union generals. In 1814, several legislatures, the Massachusetts legislature in the lead, were arranging a convention to propose far-reaching changes in the Constitution of the United States, and many feared that the outcome would be the disruption of the Union and a separate New England confederation. True, New England men were fighting bravely by land and sea for their country, but the leading Federalists of New England were, as a rule, disaffected. A notable exception was John Quincy Adams, who, distrusting the leaders of his own party, had gone over to the party of Jefferson.

The time was now come for the Southwest, the region so long distrusted, to show whether or not it was loyal to the Union. The British were aiming at that quarter a powerful military and naval force. Evidently believing the stories of disaffection in the Southwest, they had sent ahead of their expedition printed invitations to the Southwestern people to throw off the yoke of the Union.

The Spaniards of the Gulf coast, probably not ignorant of the American designs on both the Floridas, and resenting the seizure of Mobile, were no better than passive allies of the British, who were thus enabled to use Pensacola as a base for their campaign against Mobile, New Orleans, and the great Mississippi Valley beyond.

When Jackson reached Mobile, in the middle of August, he was already thoroughly angered with the Spaniards for harboring refugee Creeks and giving them arms. He had always been in favor of seizing the Floridas; that had been the real object of the expedition down the Mississippi in 1813 which he had commanded. The true reason why he and his army were dismissed at Natchez was that the authorities at Washington had changed their mind about seizing West Florida. In July, 1814, he wrote to Washington for permission to take Pensacola, but no reply came, for the War Department was occupied with General Ross. The absurd conduct of a British officer, Colonel Nichols, who was at Pensacola with a force of British and Indians, occupying one of the two Spanish forts there, and issuing fiery proclamations, was enough to make Jackson act at once, even if he had hesitated before. He answered the colonel's proclamations with others equally fiery. But he had to wait for troops, which were to come from the neighboring States of Tennessee, Kentucky, Georgia, and Louisiana. Meantime, in September, a British squadron made a determined attack on Fort Bowyer, at the entrance to Mobile Bay, and was repulsed, with the loss of its flagship, by Major Lawrence and a small garrison,--a gallant achievement, which made a good beginning of the campaign. At the end of October, Coffee, now a general officer, with nearly three thousand Tennesseans, reached the neighborhood of Mobile. With these, and about a thousand of the regulars he had already, Jackson promptly marched on Pensacola. One of the forts, and the city itself, he took; the other fort, Barrancas, was blown up by the British before he could reach it. The enterprise kept him but a week. It was all over before he received, in reply to his own letter of July, a letter from the Secretary of War forbidding him to attack Pensacola. Once again he had taken the responsibility to do what he felt to be necessary.

By this time the government at Washington was alive to the great danger of the Southwest. Hurried orders were sent to the governors of the various States whose militia must be the main reliance for defence. It was suspected that New Orleans would be the first objective of the enemy, and a warning came to the city from Jean Lafitte, the leader of a gang of smugglers, whom the British had tried to win over. But the warning was not properly heeded, and Jackson himself was slow to make up his mind where the enemy would strike. He lingered at Mobile until November 22, and four days later Sir Edward Pakenham, with a large army and a great fleet, sailed from Jamaica for New Orleans. It was not until December 2 that a worn, thin man, tired and ill, whom nobody, failing to observe the look in his eyes, would have taken for the conqueror of the Creeks, rode into the curious little city that had been the French and then the Spanish capital of Louisiana, and which was not yet half like an American town. The bulk of its population was still French Creole and African; but among the Americans there was at least one man who already knew something of Andrew Jackson, and who was to know a great deal more. The leader of the New Orleans bar, and the most active of all the citizens in making ready for the enemy, was no other than that Edward Livingston, who, with Duane and Burr, had been friendly to the Tennessee Congressman eighteen years before at Philadelphia. He invited the new commander to his house, where Mrs. Livingston, a social leader in the town, soon discovered that the Indian fighter knew perfectly well how to deport himself in a drawing-room.

IV

NEW ORLEANS

A glance at the map will give the reader some idea of the doubts that must have beset Jackson concerning the point at which the enemy would probably attack New Orleans. The island on which the city stands was accessible from the sea by at least three general routes. The British might approach by the Mississippi River, which flows by the city on the west, or over Lake Pontchartrain, which stretches out to the north, or over Lake Borgne, from the southeast. Jackson first inspected Fort St. Philip, sixty miles below, on the river; besides the fort, there were, for river defences, the schooner Carolina and the sloop Louisiana. His next move was to Lake Pontchartrain, and he was still in that quarter when news came that the enemy had chosen the third route and was already on Lake Borgne. The British found there six American gun-boats, which were all destroyed or taken after a brief but gallant struggle. That was December 14, and New Orleans was not yet in any good posture of defence. The most natural route from the lake to the immediate neighborhood of the city was up the Bayou Bienvenu, which led to the southern end of a level plain bounded on the west by the river and on the east by a dense cypress swamp. At the northern end of the plain lay New Orleans, and the distance was but six or seven miles; the plain was in most places about a mile wide. Between the head of the bayou and the city there was not a fort or even a line of intrenchments. For this state of things Jackson has not escaped blame from military critics.

But if illness or any other cause had robbed him of his usual energy, the news of the disaster on Lake Borgne was the signal for a change in him and in the situation. Coffee, with part of the Tennessee volunteers, was up the river at Baton Rouge. A hurried summons brought him a hundred and twenty miles in two days, and on the 19th he was in camp a few miles above the city with eight hundred men. Two days later came General Carroll and a brigade of Tennessee militia, two thousand strong; with them came also a squadron of mounted Mississippi volunteers. Louisiana furnished a thousand militia; the city of New Orleans five or six hundred volunteers, of whom about a third were mulattoes. Jackson had also two incomplete regiments of regulars numbering together about eight hundred rank and file. A Kentucky brigade of twenty-five hundred men was on the way, but without arms. Of Carroll's men, only one in ten had a musket. To provide arms for these new troops was a difficult matter, and many of the Kentuckians were still unarmed when the final struggle came. The city became panic-stricken and disorderly, and Jackson promptly placed it under martial law.

Such was the situation when, on the morning of December 23, the British advance party, numbering about seventeen hundred, conveyed in small boats over the shallow Lake Borgne and up the Bienvenu, landed six miles below the city and seized the mansion of Major Viller? a Creole gentleman of the neighborhood. Viller?was captured, but escaped, and at half past one o'clock Jackson knew in New Orleans that the enemy was at hand. By good luck, Major Latour, a French engineer, and the best historian of the campaign, was among the first to view the invaders, and he gave the general a correct idea of their position and numbers. As in all other crises, Jackson's resolve was taken at once. "By the Eternal," he exclaimed, "they shall not sleep on our soil!" He set his troops in motion for a night attack.

Had the British marched on to New Orleans without stopping, it seems probable that they would have taken it that evening. But at nightfall upwards of two thousand Americans were between them and the city. Jackson was on the American right, near the river, with the regulars and the Louisiana contingent. Coffee, with his Tennesseans and the Mississippi horsemen, was on the left, next the cypress swamp. Carroll's brigade and the city militia were left to guard New Orleans on the north. The Carolina had crept down the river opposite the enemy's position, and at half past seven one of her guns gave the signal for attack.

What followed, in the fog and darkness, is not clearly known. The British were surprised; but British soldiers are proverbially hard to drive from their own position. The Americans had the advantage of making the attack; but they were nearly all raw troops. Each side was confused and uncertain of its own and the enemy's position. Coffee, on the left, drove the British back towards the river, where they were protected by an old levee, while the new levee on the bank shielded them from the Louisiana's fire. On the right, the Americans were repulsed. Reinforcements reached the British army during the action. At half past nine the attack ceased. The enemy lost two hundred and sixty-seven killed, wounded, and missing; the Americans, two hundred and thirteen. The night attack, however, strengthened the Americans. The enemy, overrating Jackson's force, became too cautious to advance at once, but waited until the entire army should be landed. The Americans gained time to build defenses.

Jackson chose a line two miles above the battlefield, marked by a shallow canal or ditch which crossed the plain at its narrowest point, from the swamp to the river. Behind the ditch he threw up a parapet. In some places cotton bales were used, for the soil was but three feet deep; at that depth one found water, as indeed one found water almost everywhere,--in the foggy air, in the bayous, the river, the swamps, of that low land about New Orleans. In a few days Jackson's arrangements for defence were completed. Fifteen guns were disposed at intervals along the line, some of them manned by Lafitte and his buccaneers. The whole force numbered about three thousand, and the Kentuckians, though not all armed, were used as a reserve. On the river the Louisiana and the Carolina gave the enemy much trouble.

The British army, when completely disembarked, seemed to justify the Duke of Wellington's confidence that it could rout any American army he ever heard of. Seven thousand trained British soldiers, seamen, and marines, and a thousand West Indian blacks, were assembled at Viller?s plantation, with from twenty-five to thirty guns. There were regiments which had helped Wellington to win Talavera, Salamanca, and Vitoria, and within a few short months some of these same regiments were to stand at Waterloo in that thin red line which Ney and Napoleon's guard could never break. Their general, Pakenham, Wellington's brother-in-law, was a distinguished pupil of his illustrious kinsman. Could frontiersmen who had never fought together before, who had never seen the face of a civilized foe, withstand the conquerors of Napoleon? But two branches of the same stubborn race were represented on that little watery plain. The soldiers trained to serve the strongest will in the Old World were face to face with the rough and ready yeomanry embattled for defence by the one man of the New World whose soul had most of iron in it. It was Salamanca against Tohopeka, discipline against individual alertness, the Briton of the little Isle against the Briton of the wastes and wilds. But there was one great difference. Wellington, "the Iron Duke," was not there; "Old Hickory" was everywhere along the American lines. A grave and moderate historian, comparing the defense of New Orleans with the defence of Washington, finds the two situations not unlike. "The principal difference," he remarks, "was that Jackson commanded."

Pakenham's first concern was to get rid of the Carolina and the Louisiana. Heavy guns were with great labor hauled from the fleet, and on December 27 the Carolina's crew were forced to abandon her, and the Louisiana was with difficulty got out of range; but meanwhile Commodore Patterson had mounted a battery across the river which in a measure made up for the ships. On the 28th, Pakenham advanced with his whole army, but retired, without making any assault, to await the result of an artillery duel. This was fought on New Year's day, 1815. The British used at least twenty-four guns, throwing some three hundred and fifty pounds of metal; the Americans, fifteen guns, throwing two hundred and twenty-four pounds. On both sides novel defences were employed,--cotton bales by the Americans, barrels of sugar by the British. The bales quickly caught fire, and from that time were discarded; the barrels proved as useless as if they had been empty. The result of the action would have been utterly surprising but for the discovery already made in Canada that Americans were better marksmen than British regulars. Three American guns were damaged; every one of the British batteries was silenced and abandoned. The American loss was thirty-four killed and wounded; the British, somewhat heavier.

Pakenham waited a week for General Lambert to come up with two of his regiments, and then made his supreme effort. His plan was to advance on both sides of the river. During the night of January 7, Colonel Thornton, with 1200 men, was thrown across to the left bank, where General David Morgan had 450 Louisiana militia, reinforced at the last moment by four hundred Kentuckians. Both British divisions were to attack before dawn. But the dawn came before Thornton was ready. He was, however, successful in his part of the programme. Morgan was driven back, his guns taken, and the British on the west bank passed up the river a mile beyond Jackson's line. Jackson never forgave the Kentuckians, although military critics incline to think they did all that should have been expected.

But on the east bank it was a different story. At six o'clock the main body of the British rushed upon the American lines. General Gibbs, with 2200, sought to pierce the defenses near the swamp. General Keane led 1200 along the river bank. General Lambert, with the reserve, brought up the rear. The whole force engaged was over 5000. Gibbs first came under the American fire. The head of his division melted before it. Gibbs himself fell, mortally wounded. Pakenham, dashing forward to rally the column, was killed three hundred yards from the lines. Keane, on the British left, was wounded and carried from the field. Nowhere did the enemy pierce or break the line of defense. A brave major did indeed cross the ditch and lift his head above the breastworks; but he lived only long enough to send back word that he died on the parapet like an English soldier. In truth, Pakenham's assault was a desperate venture, such as British commanders, relying on the valor of their men, have been too often led to make. At eight o'clock Jackson walked from end to end of his works, and not a British soldier was anywhere to be seen in an attitude of offence. The smoke of the artillery, clearing, discovered the enemy far distant, in full retreat to his camp, and the battlefield littered with piles of dead and wounded. "I saw," said Jackson, "more than five hundred Britons emerging from the heaps of their dead comrades, all over the plain, rising up, and still more distinctly visible as the field became clearer, coming forward and surrendering to our soldiers."

Here was revenge, indeed, for the sufferings of little Andy in the Waxhaws, for the sabre cut on his head, for his brothers, for his mother. But it is not known that any low word of vengeance passed his lips at the awful sight before him. The British dead were seven hundred, their wounded twice as many, and five hundred were taken. In the American lines on that side of the river eight were killed and thirteen wounded. Such a victory, so cheaply bought, is not paralleled in the warfare of civilized men. Lambert, succeeding Pakenham, recalled Thornton and gave up the important advantage the British won on the western bank. For ten days the armies lay as they were, and then the enemy withdrew as he had come. A few days later, Fort Bowyer, on Mobile Point, was taken, and then the fighting ceased.

During the closing weeks of January, by the slow methods of travel prevalent in those days, three messengers were hastening to Washington with tidings which the wearied President awaited with eagerness or fear according to the quarter from which they came. From Hartford, Conn., where the convention of New England malcontents had sat, he was to learn what demands were made by Americans who chose a time of war to change and weaken, if not indeed to destroy, the constitution of their country. From the American commissioners at Ghent he hoped against hope for news of a peace. To the Southwest he looked with dread, for few had dared to believe that New Orleans could be defended. The three messages arrived almost together, and all three were to stick in men's minds for years to come, and to mould men's thoughts about their country. From Ghent came tidings of a peace, not, indeed, glorious, or such as we had gone to war to win, but better than we had a right to expect. From New Orleans, tidings of a victory so splendid that it stirred the blood and brightened the eyes of every true American, and made it hard to remember that the war had not been altogether glorious. The threatening message from Hartford lost its terrors. In the great balance of the sections, the Northeast sank, the Southwest rose. When men recalled the war with shame, it was because of Hartford; when they spoke of it with pride, as in time they came to do, it was because they saw, on the parapet of New Orleans, looking out over heaps of British dead, the thin, tall figure of the horseman in Lafayette Square. True, the victory might seem worthless, for the peace was made before the battle was fought; but the victor had won for his countrymen something dearer than anything set forth in treaties. He had won them back their good opinion of themselves. In the prosperous years that were to follow, Andrew Jackson, the man of the Southwest, was to stand as no other man could for the American's faith in his country against the world.

But the victorious general was still the same Andrew Jackson; he did not leave New Orleans without exhibiting some of the characteristics that were so well known in Tennessee. Relaxing none of his vigilance, he kept the city under martial law after the British had sailed, and even after the British admiral had sent him word of the peace. Many New Orleans people protested, and certain of them claimed exemption from the work of defense on the ground that they were citizens of France. All such he ordered out of the city. Mr. Louaillier, a leading citizen, published a protest, and Jackson promptly arrested him. Judge Hall, of the United States District Court, issued a writ of habeas corpus for the prisoner, and Jackson as promptly arrested the judge himself, and did not release him until, early in March, official notice of the peace was received. The judge fined the general a thousand dollars for contempt of court, and nearly thirty years afterwards the American Congress voted money enough to repay the sum with interest. Between the battle and the news of peace, Jackson also signed the order for the execution of six militiamen whom a court-martial had found guilty of mutiny and desertion. There were circumstances which seemed to recommend these men to mercy, and in after years the order was cited along with other things to prove that Jackson was a cruel and arbitrary commander.

However, the War Department gave him only the mildest of reproofs for his treatment of the civil authorities at New Orleans, and when he returned to Tennessee it was to a welcome even more heartfelt and stirring than the one he got on his return from the Creek war. In the autumn he was called to Washington to consult with his superiors about putting the army on a peace footing, and on the journey and at the capital he was universally received as the hero of the war. The army was reduced to ten thousand men, and distributed into a northern and a southern department. The command of the northern department was given to General Jacob Brown; Jackson got the southern department.

It was about this time that Governor Alston, of South Carolina, got a letter from his father-in-law, Aaron Burr, of New York, concerning the approaching presidential election. Burr thought Monroe, the leading candidate and the man preferred by President Madison, too weak a man for the great office. He wanted a man of firmness and decision, and he added, "that man is Andrew Jackson." But as yet Jackson himself had no such ambition. As late as 1821, in fact, he said, in reply to a suggestion that he might be President: "No, sir; I know what I am fit for. I can command a body of men in a rough way; but I am not fit to be President." He cordially supported Monroe in 1816, and after his election wrote to him and made a few suggestions about his administration. One of these suggestions was to appoint a Federalist, Colonel William Drayton, Secretary of War. Jackson declared that, had he been in command in New England, he would have hanged the leaders of the Hartford Convention; but he was in favor of recognizing the loyalty of such Federalists as had served the country faithfully during the war. That letter to Monroe was "copied" for the general by his neighbor and friend, William B. Lewis, as were hundreds of others. The general himself was a poor writer, and Major Lewis was a skilful man with a pen. He was also an exceedingly clever politician, and he showed his cleverness by keeping a second copy of the letter to Monroe for future use. In the course of the correspondence, Monroe let Jackson know that he himself might be Secretary of War if he chose; but Jackson was content with his command.

V

THE SEMINOLES AND THE POLITICIANS

For three years General Jackson was mainly occupied with the duties of a military officer in time of peace; but he was also employed to make treaties with several Indian tribes, and won another royal welcome home from the Tennesseans by throwing open to settlement large areas of Indian lands. Even in peace, however, he found an opportunity to display his readiness to do the right thing in a way to make trouble. Being several times annoyed by orders issued direct from the War Department to his inferiors, and seeing clearly that this was not the proper procedure, he issued a general order forbidding his subordinates to obey any commands which did not reach them through him. Calhoun, who became Secretary of War soon afterwards, conceded the justice of the general's position, but Jackson's course in the matter was certainly rather high-handed. General Winfield Scott criticised it in private conversation, and a mischief-maker brought his words to Jackson's attention. The result was some fiery and abusive letters to Scott, and a challenge to a duel, which Scott, on religious grounds, very properly declined.

Jackson also carried on an angry correspondence with General Adair, of Kentucky, who defended the Kentucky troops from the charge of cowardice at New Orleans.

It was late in the year 1817 before General Jackson was again called to active service in the field. Once more the call was from the southward, and his old enemies, the Red Sticks, the English, and the Spaniards, were all in some measure responsible for it. A number of Red Sticks had taken refuge with their kinsmen, the Seminoles, in Florida. Colonel Nichols and a small force of British had also remained in Florida some time after the war ended, and had done things of a nature to stir up the Indians there against the Americans across the border. Negro slaves, escaping from American masters, had fled to the Spanish province in considerable numbers, and a body of them got possession of a fort on the Apalachicola River which had been abandoned by the British. To add to the disorder of the province, it was frequented by adventurers, some of them claiming to be there in order to lead a revolution against Spain, some of them probably mere freebooters. The Spanish authorities at Pensacola were too weak to control such a population, and Americans near the border were anxious to have their government interfere. The negro fort was a centre of lawlessness, and some American troops marched down the river, bombarded it, and by a lucky shot blew up its magazine and killed nearly three hundred negroes. Troubles arose with the Indians also, and Fowltown, an Indian village, was taken and burned. A considerable body of Indians took to the war-path, and Jackson was ordered to the scene.

Impatient as ever with the Spaniards, he wrote to President Monroe: "Let it be signified to me through any channel (say Mr. J. Rhea) that the possession of Florida would be desirable to the United States, and in sixty days it will be accomplished." Monroe was ill at the time, and for some reason did not attend to the general's letter for a year. The President was trying to get Florida peaceably, by purchase, and not by conquest. Jackson, however, got the idea that his suggestion was approved, and acted accordingly.

Raising troops in Tennessee on his own authority, he marched rapidly to the scene of trouble, crossed the border into Florida, and in a few weeks crushed the Seminoles. Of fighting, in fact, there was very little; what there was fell almost entirely to the friendly Indians, and not a single American soldier was killed. But Jackson's actions in the campaign brought on the bitterest controversies of his career. By his order four men were put to death, and he captured Pensacola again, claiming that some Indians had taken refuge there. Two of the four men were Creek Red Sticks. The other two were white men and British subjects. One was Alexander Arbuthnot, an old man of seventy, a trader among the Indians, and, so far as is known, a man of good character. He was taken prisoner, however, and it is supposed a letter he wrote to his son, telling him to take their merchandise to a place of safety, warned some Indians of Jackson's approach. The other British subject was an Englishman named Robert Ambrister, who had been a lieutenant in the British army. He was nephew to the governor of New Providence, one of the British West Indies, and seems to have been in Florida rather in search of adventure than for any clearly ascertainable purpose. A court-martial found Arbuthnot guilty of inciting the Creek Indians to rise against the United States, and of aiding the enemy. Ambrister was found guilty of levying war against the United States. He was first sentenced to be shot; then, on reconsideration, the court changed the sentence to fifty stripes and hard labor for a year. Jackson firmly believed that both were British emissaries, sent to Florida to stir up the Indians. He disapproved the change of Ambrister's sentence, and ordered him to be shot and Arbuthnot to be hanged.

Such fierce and energetic measures, whether justifiable or not, put an end to the disorder on the border, and Jackson was again free to return home a victor. The country was disposed to approve what he had done, but the President and Cabinet saw that grave international questions would be raised; for Jackson had invaded the soil of a country at peace with the United States, taken possession of its forts, and put to death citizens of another country also at peace with the United States. John C. Calhoun, of South Carolina, the Secretary of War, was in favor of censuring the general for his conduct; but John Quincy Adams, of Massachusetts, the Secretary of State, thought his acts necessary under the circumstances, and declared himself ready to defend them. In the end he did defend them so well that neither Spain nor Great Britain made serious trouble over them. The President and his Cabinet followed Adams's advice instead of Calhoun's, and Calhoun himself, as Jackson's superior, wrote to him about the campaign in a friendly way. Jackson naturally thought that Calhoun had been his friend in the Cabinet, and had no reason to suspect that it was Adams who defended, and Calhoun who wished to censure him. He did not learn the truth for many years. Had he known it sooner, there is no telling how different the political history of the next twenty years might have been.

For henceforth Jackson was to be a great figure not in warfare but in politics. His military career was practically ended. He kept his commission until July, 1821, but from this time he fought no more battles. He had not, as a soldier, given such evidence of military genius as to set his name alongside those of the great captains of history, but he had shown himself a strong and successful leader of men; in his masterful, often irregular and violent way, he had done his country good service. Were his place in history merely a soldier's, it would be a safe one, though not the highest. But his actions in the field soon gave him the leading part on a different stage. One day in January, 1819, he rode up to the house of his neighbor, Major Lewis, who had just bought a new overcoat, and asked him to get himself another; the general wanted the one already made to wear on a long journey. "Major," he said, "there is a combination in Washington to ruin me. I start to Washington tomorrow."

The chief of those who, as Jackson firmly believed, were combined to ruin him, was the man who could with best reason be compared to the hero of New Orleans for the place he had in the affections of the Western people and as the representative of the new American spirit, born of the second war with Great Britain. If Jackson was the hero of the war, Henry Clay was its orator; if it was Jackson who sent from one quarter the news of a glorious victory, it was Clay who, with Adams and Gallatin, had secured the peace. Leaving Ghent, Clay was lingering in Paris when he heard the news of New Orleans.

"Now," he exclaimed, "I can go to England without mortification." But the great orator was not in sympathy with Monroe's administration. His enemies declared he was in opposition because he was not asked to be Secretary of State, and because he feared that Adams, who had the place, would become President four years later. However that may have been, it was Clay who led the attack on the administration about the campaign in Florida. Protesting his deep respect for "the illustrious military chieftain" who commanded there, he yet condemned the hanging of the two Red Sticks, the execution of Arbuthnot and Ambrister, the taking of Pensacola.

From the moment Jackson read that speech he was Clay's enemy, and a warfare began that lasted twenty-five years. Every man, in fact, who in the course of the long debate that followed condemned the acts of General Jackson in Florida was written down an enemy on the tablets of his memory. He remained in Washington until the House had voted down every resolution unfavorable to his course, and he had thus won his first victory over Clay. Then he set forth on a northern journey which showed him the immense popularity he had in places like New York, Philadelphia, and Baltimore, and gave him an opportunity to increase it by the fine appearance he made in public. He returned to find that a Senate committee had reported unfavorably on his conduct, but the Senate never acted on the report, and on his journey homeward the people gave him every reason to believe that the great majority of his countrymen approved the votes of the lower house. As if to complete his triumph, he was soon called once more to Florida; and this time he entered Pensacola, not as a soldier invading a foreign province, but as the chief magistrate of an American territory. In February, 1821, after so many years of negotiation, Florida was bought by the United States. President Monroe appointed Jackson governor and commissioner to receive the province, and he, bidding farewell to the army, entered again upon the duties of a civil office.

Even in his farewell to his troops, Jackson took occasion to attack a policy recently favored by his superior, General Jacob Brown, and any one who knew Jackson might have guessed that the holding of a civil office would never keep him from violent courses, particularly in Pensacola. He held the office only a few months, for he was in wretched health. His wife, who was with him, tells in one of her letters how pale and solemn he was when he rode into Pensacola for the third time, and how ill he was while he was there. He resigned in October, but before he resigned he had made another cause of dispute with Spain. The retiring Spanish governor, Callava, was accused of attempting to carry away papers which were necessary to establish the property rights of a quadroon family. The correspondence on the subject led to a series of misunderstandings, and General Jackson was soon convinced that villainy was afoot. The upshot of the dispute was that the American governor put the Spanish governor in jail; and when the United States judge of West Florida, a curious character named Fromentin, tried to mend the matter with a writ of habeas corpus, he fared little better than Judge Hall of New Orleans had fared before him.

Mr. Parton's laborious investigation of this comical affair enables him to show that the estate over which the trouble arose was of no value whatever, and that Jackson's chivalrous impulse to defend a family he thought wronged led him into a very arbitrary and indefensible action. As usual, his motives were good, but his temper was not improved by his illness or by the fact that Callava, who seems to have been a worthy gentleman, was a Spaniard, and had been governor of Florida. Jackson had a rooted dislike of Spanish governors, and doubtless congratulated himself and the country that there would be no more of them in Florida, when, for the last time, he turned northward from Pensacola to seek The Hermitage and the rest which his diseased body sorely needed.

The Hermitage was by this time a good place to rest in, for it had grown to be a Southern plantation home, quite unlike the bare homes which sheltered the first settlers of that neighborhood, and it had its full share of the charm that belonged to that old Southern life. It was the seat of an abundant hospitality. The fame of its master drew thither interesting men from a distance. His benevolence, and the homely charity of his wife, made it a resort for many of the neighborhood whom they two had befriended, for young people fond of the simple amusements of those days, and for ministers of the Gospel, whom Mrs. Jackson, an extremely pious woman, liked especially to have about her. For his wife's sake, the general built a tiny church on the estate, and always treated with profound respect the religion which he himself had not professed, but which he honored because Mrs. Jackson was a Christian. Indeed, there is nothing in the man's whole life more honorable than his perfect loyalty to her. She was a simple, uncultivated, kind-hearted frontier woman, no longer attractive in person, and a great contrast to the courtly figure by her side when she and the general were in company. It is certainly true that the two used to smoke their reed pipes together before the fire after dinner, and that custom, to one ignorant of American life in the Southwest, would stamp them as persons of the lowest manners. Yet it is also true that "Aunt Rachel," as Mrs. Jackson was commonly called by younger people of the neighborhood, was loved and honored by all who knew her. The general had not merely fine manners, but that which is finer far than the finest manners: he had kindness for his slaves, hospitality for strangers, gentleness with women and children. Lafayette was at The Hermitage in 1825, and his noble nature was drawn to Jackson in a way quite impossible to understand if he was nothing more than the vindictive duelist, the headstrong brawler, the crusher out of Indians, the hater of Britons and Spaniards, which we know that he was. Lafayette found at The Hermitage the pistols which he himself had given to Washington and which, with many swords and other tokens of the public esteem, had come to the hero of New Orleans. The friend of Washington declared that the pistols had come to worthy hands, notwithstanding that his host was equally ready to display another weapon with the remark, "That is the pistol with which I killed Mr. Dickinson."

It seems clear that Jackson honestly meant to spend the rest of his days at the Hermitage. His friend Eaton, a Senator from Tennessee, had already written his life down to New Orleans, and probably he would have been content, so far as his public career was concerned, to let finis follow the name of his greatest victory. But Eaton himself, and Major Lewis, and other friends, and the vast public which his deeds had stirred, would not let him alone.

Within a year of his retirement, a group of his friends were working shrewdly to make him President of the United States. In 1823, John Williams, who was an enemy to Jackson, came before the Tennessee legislature for reelection to the United States Senate. Jackson's friends were determined to beat him, and found they could do it in only one way. They elected Jackson himself. In that, as in all the clever political work that was done for him, Major Lewis was the leading man. Before the time came to choose a successor to President Monroe in 1824, Tennessee had declared for her foremost citizen, and Pennsylvania, to the surprise of the country, soon followed the lead. The sceptre was about to pass from the Virginian line, and from all the great sections of the Union distinguished statesmen stepped forward to grasp it. From Georgia came William H. Crawford, a practiced politician; from South Carolina, John C. Calhoun, the subtlest of reasoners; from Kentucky, Henry Clay, the orator; from Massachusetts, John Quincy Adams, the best trained of public servants. Only Tennessee offered a soldier.

It was twenty-six years from the end of Jackson's first service in Congress to his second appearance in the Senate. Again he showed himself unfit to shine as a legislator, but in spite of that he was now clearly the most marked figure in the upper house. None of his rivals were Senators. Clay was the Speaker of the House; Adams, Crawford, and Calhoun were in the Cabinet. Jackson probably did not occupy more than ten minutes of the Senate's time during the whole session, but his fame and his candidacy made his votes on the tariff and internal improvements important data to politicians. The country was already entered upon the second period of its history, in which there was to be no French party and no English party; in which a voter should choose his party on account of its position on such questions as the tariff, internal improvements, and the bank, or on account of the general view of the Constitution which it favored. But as yet no clear division into such parties had come about. The old Federalist party was no longer in the field, and no other had arisen to take its place. It was a time of personal politics. The first question was, Who is to succeed Monroe? and the next question, Who is to succeed the successor of Monroe?

Jackson found some firm friends awaiting him in Washington, and he soon added to their number by becoming reconciled to some old enemies. Among the old friends was Livingston, now Congressman from Louisiana. One of the old enemies was the Senator from Missouri, whose chair was next his own; for the Senator from Missouri, a rising man in Washington, was Thomas H. Benton. According to Benton's account, Jackson made the first advance, and they were soon on friendly terms, though Benton continued to support Clay, whose niece he had married. General Winfield Scott made an overture, and Jackson cordially responded. Even with Henry Clay he was induced by mutual friends to stand on a footing of courteous friendliness, though there never was any genuine friendship between them.

Against Crawford, the Georgian candidate, and at first the leading candidate of all, he had a grudge that dated from 1815. Crawford was Secretary of War at that time, and, contrary to Jackson's advice, had restored to the Cherokees certain lands which Jackson had got from the Creeks by the treaty of Fort Jackson, but which the Cherokees claimed. When Crawford offered himself against Monroe in 1816, Jackson was ardently for the Virginian; and now, when it was apparent that the caucus of Republican Senators and Representatives would probably nominate Crawford, Jackson's friends joined the friends of other candidates in opposing the caucus altogether, so that in the end only sixty-six persons attended it, and its action was deprived of the weight it had formerly had in presidential contests. Before the election, Crawford was stricken with paralysis, and this greatly weakened his chances.

Both Calhoun and Adams were on friendly terms with Jackson. Jackson still supposed that Calhoun had defended the Florida campaign in the Cabinet. His good feeling toward the South Carolinian was doubtless strengthened when Calhoun, who had relied on the support of Pennsylvania, gracefully yielded to Jackson's superior popularity in that quarter, and withdrew from the contest. It was then generally agreed that he should be Vice-President, and probably General Jackson, like many others, was willing that he should restore the old order of things according to which the Vice-President, instead of the Secretary of State, stood in line of succession to the presidency.

Adams was Secretary of State, and as such he had rendered Jackson important services by defending his actions in Florida. Adams, in diplomacy, believed in standing up for his own country quite as resolutely as the frontier general did in war. Nor were they far apart on the tariff and internal improvements, the domestic questions of the day. Adams's diary for this period shows a good feeling for Jackson. In honor of the general, Mrs. Adams gave a great ball January 8, 1824, the anniversary of New Orleans.

The election turned, as so many others have turned, on the vote of New York, which Martin Van Buren, an astute politician, was trying to carry for Crawford. He did not succeed, and there was no choice by the people. Jackson led with ninety-nine votes in the electoral college; Adams had eighty-four, Crawford forty-one, Clay thirty-seven. In some States the electors were still chosen by the legislature. Outside of those States Jackson had fifty thousand more votes than Adams, and Adams's vote was nearly equal to Crawford's and Clay's combined. For Vice-President, Calhoun had a large majority.

Under the Constitution, the House of Representatives had now to choose a President from the three leading candidates. Clay was Speaker, and had great influence over the House, but his own name had to be dropped. Beaten himself, he had the power to make any one of his three rivals President of the United States.

It was a trying situation for him and for the three citizens whose fate he seemed to hold in his hands. Crawford was so ill that Clay could not seriously consider him. Adams had never liked Clay, though they generally agreed about public questions, and the ardent Kentuckian could never have found the cold manners of the New England statesman attractive. But from the first he preferred Adams to Jackson, thinking a mere "military chieftain" unfit for the office. On the 9th of February, Adams was elected. That evening he and Jackson met at a presidential reception. Of the two, the defeated Westerner bore himself far more graciously than the successful candidate from New

England.

Up to this time, no unseemly conduct could be charged against any one of the four rivals. But the human nature of these men could not bear to the end the strain of such a rivalry. For many years the jealousy and hatred and suspicion it gave birth to were to blacken American politics. Jackson was guilty of a grave injustice to Clay and Adams; and they, by a political blunder, delivered themselves into his hands. Jackson and his friends charged them with "bargain and corruption." Adams, by appointing Clay Secretary of State, and Clay, by accepting the office, gave their enemies the only evidence they ever had to offer of the truth of the charge. Every other semblance of a proof was shown to be worthless, and the characters of the two men have convinced all candid historians that the charge was false. But there was no way to prove that the charge was false. Jackson believed it, and from this time he made war on Clay and Adams. He believed he had a wrong to right, a combination of scoundrelly enemies to overthrow, a corrupted government to purify and save. The election had shown him to be the most popular of all the candidates, and his friends, of whom Benton was now the foremost, contended that the House ought to have chosen him in obedience to the people's will. Until he should be elected, he and his followers seemed to feel that the people were hoodwinked by the politicians.

Hitherto, since his second entrance into public life, he had borne himself as became a soldier whose battles were already fought. Webster had written of him: "General Jackson's manners are more presidential than those of any other candidate. He is grave, mild, and reserved." But now he was once more the Jackson of the tavern brawl, of the Dickinson duel. Politics had come to be a fight, and his friends had no more need to urge him on. He resigned his place in the Senate, and was at once, for the second time, nominated for President by the Tennessee legislature. With untiring industry and great political shrewdness, Lewis, Eaton, Benton, Livingston, and others of his friends set to work to get him elected. The campaign of 1824 was no sooner ended than the campaign of 1828 was begun.

It was an important campaign because it went far to divide the old Republican party, to which all the candidates of 1824 had belonged, into the two parties which were to battle for supremacy throughout the next quarter of a century. The division was partly a matter of principles and policies, but it was also a matter of organization.

As to principles and measures, Adams was disposed to revive those policies which the old Federalist party had adopted in the days of its power. He had left that party in 1808, not because he had given up its early principles, but because he believed that its leaders, particularly in New England, in their bitter opposition to Jefferson, had gone to the point where opposition to the party in power passes into disloyalty to the country. In the Republican party he always acted with those men who, like Henry Clay, favored a strong government at Washington and looked with distrust on any attempt of a State to set up its own powers against the powers of the United States. As President, he wished the government to take vigorous measures for defense, for developing the country by internal improvements, for protecting American industries by heavy duties on goods imported from other countries. He thought that the public lands should be sold at the highest prices they would bring, and the money used by the general government to promote the public welfare. He had no doubt as to the government's power to maintain a national bank, and thought that was the very best way to manage the finances.

Jackson himself was not a free-trader, and had committed himself to a "proper" tariff on protection lines; but during the campaign he was made to appear less of a tariff man than Adams. He had also voted for certain national roads and other internal improvements, but he had not committed himself sweepingly to that policy. He doubted the constitutionality of a national bank. As to the public lands, he favored a liberal policy, with the object of developing the western country by attracting settlers rather than raising money to be spent by the government. On the general question of the powers of the government he stood for a stricter construction of the Constitution and greater respect for the rights of the States than Adams believed in. So, notwithstanding Jackson's tariff views, the mass of the people held him a better representative of Jeffersonian Democracy than his rival.

But a party is an organization, and not merely a list of principles. It is, as some one has said, a crowd, and not merely a creed. Jackson's managers so organized his supporters that they became a party in that sense much more clearly than in the sense of holding the same views. Committees were formed all over the country somewhat on the order of the committees of correspondence of Revolutionary times. Newspapers were set up to attack the administration and hold the Jackson men together. Everywhere Jackson was represented as the candidate of the plain people against the politicians. In all such work Major Lewis was active and shrewd, and before the end of the campaign, from another quarter of the union, Jackson won a recruit who was already a past master in all the lore of party politics. Martin Van Buren was a pupil in the political school of Aaron Burr, and was recognized as the cleverest politician of a State in which the sort of politics that is concerned with securing elections rather than fighting for principles had grown into a science and an art. New York was then thought a doubtful State, and the support of Van Buren was of the utmost value.

It is probable that so far as Adams and Jackson differed on questions of principle and policy, a majority of the people were with Jackson. But it is also clear that the campaign was fought out as a sort of personal contest between the Southwestern soldier and the two statesmen whom he accused of bargain and corruption. It was a campaign of bitter personal abuse on both sides. Adams, perhaps the most rigidly conscientious statesman since Washington, was accused of dishonesty, of extravagance, of riches, of debt, of betraying his old friends, the Federalists, of trying to bring Federalists back into power. Against Jackson his enemies brought up his many fights and duels, his treatment of Judge Hall and Judge Fromentin, the execution of Woods and the six militiamen, of the two Indians, of Arbuthnot and Ambrister. Handbills were distributed, each decorated with a coffin bearing the name of one of his victims. His private life was attacked. The scandal of his marriage was blazoned in newspapers and pamphlets. Even the unknown grave of his mother was not spared.

So it became largely a question of the two men, and which the people liked best. Adams, coldly virtuous, would not turn his finger to make himself better liked; even if he had attempted the arts of popularity, he was, of all the eminent men of our history, the least endowed with charm of manner, speech, and bearing. He sternly refused to appoint any man to office for supporting him, or to turn any man out of office for opposing him. He could not be winning or gracious on public occasions. Ezekiel, the shrewd old brother of Daniel Webster, wrote to him after the election that even in New England men supported Adams "from a cold sense of duty, and not from any liking of the man." It took a New England conscience to hold a follower in line for the New England candidate. The man of the Southwest won many a vote where the voter's conscience did but half consent. Wherever he went, he made bitter enemies or devoted friends, rather than cold critics and lukewarm admirers. Adams was an honest man, but nobody had ever called him "Old Hickory." He was an ardent patriot, and could point to many wise state papers he had written, to a report on weights and measures which had cost him four years of patient labor; but he could not, like his rival, journey down the Mississippi and celebrate the anniversary of a great victory in the city he had saved. His followers might ably defend his course on public questions, but what was it all worth if the people kept on shouting, "Hurrah for Jackson"?

Of all the sections of the country only New England gave Adams a solid support. Jackson swept the West and South and carried the great States of Pennsylvania and New York. In Tennessee, nineteen men out of twenty voted for him. There is a story of a traveller who reached a Tennessee town the next day and found the whole male population pursuing with tar and feathers two reckless citizens who had voted against "the general." In the electoral college he had one hundred and seventy-eight votes to Adams's eighty-three. Calhoun was again chosen Vice-President.

The poor boy had won his way to the White House, but it was a worn old man, bowed down with a heavy sorrow, who journeyed across the mountains to take the great prize. The cruel campaign scandal about his marriage had aggravated a heart trouble from which his wife had long suffered. She died in December, and his grief was appalling to those who gathered at The Hermitage to do honor to "Aunt Rachel." It was not in Jackson's nature, as indeed it would not have been in the nature of many men, to forget, in his grief, the enemies who had helped to cause it. His old age, like his youth, was to be cursed with hatred and the thought of revenge.

VI

THE WHITE HOUSE

March 4, 1829, Andrew Jackson became President of the United States. A great crowd of strange-looking men went to see him inaugurated. "They really seem to think," wrote Webster, "that the country has been rescued from some great danger." Whoever else may have thought so, Jackson certainly held that opinion. As his wont was, he saw the danger and the villainy which he thought himself commissioned to destroy in the person of a man; and that man was Henry Clay. Martin Van Buren was to succeed Clay as Secretary of State in the new Cabinet, but he did not reach Washington until after the 4th of March. Jackson accordingly sent his friend, Colonel Hamilton, of New York, to the State Department, ordering him to take charge there the instant he should hear the gun which was to announce that the new President had taken the oath of office.

Jackson and Clay were, in fact, the leaders of the two parties into which the old Republican party was now divided. Their rise to leadership meant that a new set of public men and a new set of questions had come to the front; it meant a more thoroughgoing experiment of democracy than had yet been tried in America. Adams's administration is properly considered to have been the last of one series and Jackson's the first of another. Under the earlier Presidents, national affairs were committed mainly to a few trained statesmen, the people simply approving or disapproving the men and the measures brought before them, but not of themselves putting forward candidates for the higher offices or in any wise initiating policies. The rule of the people was thus a passive sort of rule, a rule by consent. But with the wide prevalence of manhood suffrage, and the prominence of domestic questions,--of questions concerning the business and the daily life of the Republic,--and with the disappearance of the profound questions concerning the organization of the government and the nature of government in general, the people began to assert themselves. Under Jackson and his successors, they made themselves felt more and more at Washington; their opinions and sentiments, their likes and dislikes, their whims and prejudices, were projected into their government. Henceforth, public men were to be powerful not so much in proportion to their knowledge of statecraft as in proportion to their popularity. They must represent the popular will, or commend themselves and their policies to popular favor. The public men of the old order, like Adams, might be wise and faithful, but they lacked Clay's and Jackson's sympathetic understanding of the common people. And of the two new leaders Jackson had by far the stronger hold on the popular mind and heart. The people had sent him to Washington because he was of them and like them, and because they liked him. Both he and they felt that he was their President, and he held himself responsible to them only.

It seemed, too, that with the new questions and the new men there was coming a new sort of politics. Jackson meant to serve the people faithfully, but he entered upon the duties of his great office in the spirit of a victorious general. The sort of politics most in accord with his feeling was the sort of politics which prevailed in New York and Pennsylvania. Jackson once declared, "I am not a politician, but if I were, I should be a New York politician." Before long, a leading New York politician, Senator Marcy, expressed the sentiment of his fellows when he said, "To the victors belong the spoils." That was a sentiment which a soldier President could understand. In that letter to Monroe which Major Lewis wrote for him twelve years before, and which won him votes, he had urged that partisan considerations should not control appointments; but before he had been President a year he removed more men from office than all his predecessors had removed since the beginning of the government. When he left Washington, the practice of removing and appointing men for political reasons was so firmly established that the patient work of reform has not to this day destroyed it. That, to many historians, was the gravest fault of Jackson's administration. It was, however, merely New York methods applied to national politics, and it was a perfectly natural outcome of Jackson's conviction that the people had sent him there to drive out the men who had control of the government.

In fact, unless we understand President Jackson himself, we cannot possibly understand his administration; for President Jackson, though he was now somewhat subdued in manner, and "By the Eternal" was not quite so often on his lips, was still Jackson of the duelling pistol and Jackson of the sword; and he was also still the Jackson whom Benton saw with the lamb and the child between his knees. All men were still divided for him into friends and enemies. The party opposed to him came soon to call itself the National Republican Party, and later the Whig Party, while his own followers were called Democratic Republicans, or Democrats. But to Jackson the National Republicans were the friends of Henry Clay, as the Democrats were his own friends. So, too, of the great questions he had to deal with. In every case he was fighting not merely a policy or an institution but a man.

For a time, however, his arch-enemy, Clay, disappeared from the scene. Until the autumn of 1831, he was in retirement in Kentucky. Jackson had the field to himself, and was at first occupied with his friends rather than his enemies.

Van Buren, as Secretary of State, was the head of the new Cabinet. The other members were not men of great distinction. They had, however, one thing in common: in one way or another, they had all opposed Mr. Clay. On other points they differed. Half of them were friends of Calhoun, and wished to see him President after Jackson. They were also divided into married men and a widower, Mr. Van Buren being the widower. That, as things turned out, was a very important division indeed.

Jackson did not treat his Cabinet as other Presidents had treated theirs. He had a soldier's idea of organization, and did not think it necessary to consult the Cabinet members about all the measures he planned. He treated them somewhat as a general treats his inferior officers, though with several of them, especially Van Buren and Eaton, his relations were very cordial and intimate. When he wished advice, however, he was more apt to seek it of his friend, Major Lewis, whom he had persuaded to accept an appointment, and who lived with him at the White House, or of Isaac Hill, who had come to Washington after fighting the Adams men in New Hampshire, or of Amos Kendall, who had dared to oppose Clay in Kentucky, or of General Duff Green, editor of "The Telegraph," the Jackson organ. These men, personal friends of the President, came to be called the "Kitchen Cabinet;" and at least three of the four were shrewd enough to justify any President in consulting them. Hill and Kendall were both New England men by birth, and had all the industry and sharpness of mind proverbially characteristic of Yankees. Even Major Lewis did not surpass Kendall in political cleverness and far-sightedness; he was a "little whiffet of a man," but before long the opposition learned to see his hand in every event of political importance anywhere in the country. If a Democratic convention in Maine framed a resolution, or a newspaper in New Orleans changed its policy, men were ready to declare that it was Kendall who pulled the wire. Historians are fond of saying that it was such men as Kendall and Lewis who really ruled the country while Jackson was President; and it is true that by skilful suggestions, by playing upon his likes and dislikes, much could be done with him. But it is equally true that when he was once resolved on any course his friends could no more stop him than his enemies could. A clerk in the State Department won his favor by a happy use of the phrase, "I take the responsibility," and from that time was safe even against the displeasure of Secretary Van Buren. A member of Congress began a successful intrigue for office by begging for his father the pipe which the President was smoking, ashes and all. A clerk in the War Department attracted his attention by challenging a man to a duel, and so started himself on a career that ended in the Senate. Secretary Van Buren called on Peggy Eaton and supplanted Calhoun as the heir apparent to the presidency. Jackson in good humor was the easiest of victims to an artful intriguer; but, unlike the weak kings whom scheming ministers have shaped to their purposes, he could not be stopped when once he was started.

It was Peggy Eaton who made a division between the married men and the widower of the Cabinet. She was the wife of Senator Eaton, who was now Secretary of War, and the widow of a naval officer named Timberlake. Her father was a tavern-keeper named O'Neill, and both Jackson and Eaton had lived at his tavern when they were Senators, and Mrs. O'Neill had been kind to Mrs. Jackson. The O'Neills had no place in Washington society, and there were ugly stories about the conduct of Mrs. Timberlake with Senator Eaton before the death of Timberlake, who killed himself at sea. Washington society believed these stories. President Jackson refused to believe them, and became Mrs. Eaton's champion. His zeal in her cause knew no bounds, and he wished his secretaries and their wives to help him. But the Cabinet ladies would not visit or receive Mrs. Eaton, and their husbands refused to interfere. Calhoun, the Vice-President, also declined to take up Mrs. Eaton's cause. Mr. Van Buren, a widower, showed the lady marked attention.

For once in his life, Andrew Jackson was defeated. Creeks and Spaniards and Redcoats he could conquer, but the ladies of Washington never surrendered, and Peggy Eaton, though her affairs became a national question, never got into Washington society. Jackson, however, did not forget who had been his friends in a little matter any more than if it had been the greatest affair of state.

It was already a question whether Calhoun or Van Buren should lead the Jackson party at the end of the one term which Jackson had declared to be the limit of his stay in the White House. Calhoun's friends in the Cabinet, and General Duff Green, of "The Telegraph," were active in his interest. Van Buren, however, was constantly growing in favor with the President. When at last Jackson discovered that Calhoun, as a member of Monroe's Cabinet, had wished to censure him for his conduct in Florida, he and the Vice-President broke forever. Meantime, a great public question had arisen on which the two men stood out as representatives of two opposite theories of the Union.

The estrangement begun over Peggy Eaton widened into a breach between a State and the United States, between the nullifier of the laws and the defender of the Union.

For the pendulum had swung, and it was no longer the Federalist merchants of New England, but the planters of the South, and particularly of South Carolina, who were discontent with the policy of the government. New England had turned to manufactures some of the energy she had formerly given to commerce and seafaring, and was now in favor of a protective tariff. Webster, her foremost man at Washington, had voted against the tariff of 1816, but had changed his mind and supported a higher tariff in 1824, and a still higher in 1828. The planters of the South had not found it easy to develop manufactures with their slave labor. They had little or nothing, therefore, to protect against the products of European countries. On the contrary, they exported much of their cotton to England, and imported from England and other countries many of the things they consumed. Accordingly, they were, as a rule, opposed to the whole system of tariff taxation, and desired free trade. Many of them also opposed the system of internal improvements, both on constitutional grounds and because they felt that the tariff made them pay more than their share of the expense of such undertakings.

On the question of internal improvements Jackson soon took a stand entirely pleasing to the opponents of the system. In his first message to Congress he declared against it, and when Congress passed a bill subscribing money to the stock of the Maysville and Lexington road, one of the chief internal improvements so far undertaken, and an enterprise specially favored by Clay, he promptly vetoed it. Other such measures he vetoed unless it was clear that a two-thirds majority in each House would pass them over his veto. He preferred that the money received from the sale of public lands should be distributed among the States, believing that they, instead of the general government, should undertake the improvements necessary to the development of the country.

Jackson had, indeed, great respect for the rights of the States under the

Constitution, and warned Congress not to go beyond the powers which were clearly given to the general government. The State of Georgia had long been discontent because the Indians were not removed from her borders, and the President sympathized strongly with her feeling. As soon as he was elected, the Georgia legislature passed an act dividing up the Cherokee country into counties, and extending over them the civil laws of the State. The act was plainly contrary to treaties between the Indians and the Federal government, but the President refused to interfere. On the contrary, he withdrew all United States troops from the Indian country, and left the State to deal with the Indians as it chose. Later on, the Supreme Court of the United States decided that the Georgia law was unconstitutional because it took away the treaty rights of the Cherokees. "John Marshall has made his decision," said Jackson, "now let him enforce it." The President, in fact, was heartily in favor of removing the Indians, and before he went out of office the last of the Southern tribes had given up its old home for a new one in the West.

Jackson's collision with Chief Justice Marshall over this question had very far-reaching effects, which historians have somewhat neglected in their study of the consequences of his course on other questions. No statesman, no President, had done so much as the great Chief Justice to make the general government strong and to restrain the States. Jackson, disagreeing with some of Marshall's views, never lost an opportunity to put on the bench a man of his own way of thinking. The result was that many years later, when, in a great crisis, the supporters of the national government and the leaders of States about to break away from the Union looked to the Supreme Court to decide between them, the voice that came from the august tribunal spoke words which Marshall and Story would never have uttered, but which the champions of the States heard with delight.

On these important questions, then, President Jackson acted like an extreme Jeffersonian Democrat. But the South Carolinians soon found that if he was ready to keep the general government from interfering with any right that could reasonably be claimed for a State, he was equally ready to stand up for the Union when he thought a State was going too far.

He had nothing to do with the tariff of 1828. In his first message he suggested that some modifications of it were desirable, and pointed out that the public debt would soon be paid, and it would be advisable to reduce certain of the duties. But modification was too mild a word to suit the South Carolinians. The law was the outcome of the clamor of many selfish interests, and Congressmen opposed altogether to protection had helped to make it as bad as possible, hoping that it might in the end be defeated. When it passed, the South Carolina legislature vigorously protested, and began at once to debate about the best plan of resistance. The plan finally preferred was for the State to declare the law unconstitutional, and therefore null and void, and call on other States to join in the declaration. If the national government tried to enforce the law in South Carolina, she would protect her citizens, and as the final resort withdraw from the Union. The plan was first placed before the American people in an "Exposition and Protest" adopted by the South Carolina legislature in 1828; and the real author of that famous document, though the fact was not then known, was the Vice-President, Calhoun. The associate of Clay in those acts which had made a beginning of internal improvements and of protection, long a statesman of the strong-government school, Calhoun had been led by the distress and discontent of his own people to examine the Constitution again, "in order," as he said afterwards, "to ascertain fully the nature and character of our political system," and had now come to a change of views.

The nullification doctrine came before Congress in the winter of 1829-30, and was debated in the most famous of American debates. Clay was not there to speak for his tariff system, but a greater orator than Clay took up the challenge. In the greatest of all American orations since Patrick Henry spoke for liberty, Webster spoke for union and liberty, and Americans will never forget his words until liberty and union are alike destroyed. Jackson was the last man in the country to miss their force. No orator himself, he yet knew how to give words the power of a promised or a threatened deed. Not long after the debate, there was a public dinner of the States'-Rights men in Washington to celebrate Jefferson's birthday. Jackson did not attend, but he sent a toast, and probably the seven words of his toast were more confounding to the nullifiers than all the stately paragraphs of Webster's oration. It was: "Our Federal Union: it must be preserved." Calhoun's toast was: "The Union,--next to our liberties the most dear,"--and Jackson, who was just learning that he had been mistaken about Calhoun in 1818, began now to see clearly that the great South Carolinian was in sympathy with the nullifiers. Many South Carolinians, however, were still hoping that the President would not take any active measures to defeat their plan. Some of them went on hoping until the Fourth of July, 1831, when there was read, at a public dinner of Union men at Charleston, a letter from Jackson which left no doubt of what he meant to do if they kept on. He was going to enforce the laws and preserve the Union.

Having by this time broken utterly with Calhoun, he desired to rid himself of those cabinet members who were Calhoun's friends, and to that end took the bold and unexampled step of changing his cabinet entirely,--only Barry, the postmaster-general, being kept in office. Van Buren fell readily into the plan, gave up his portfolio, and was at once appointed minister to Great Britain. Edward Livingston took his place. A change in the "Kitchen Cabinet" followed. General Duff Green would not desert Calhoun, and so "The Telegraph" ceased to be the organ of the administration. Instead, Francis P. Blair, of Kentucky, who, like Amos Kendall, had been first the friend and then the enemy of Clay, was called to Washington, and set up "The Globe," which soon became a power for Jackson. Nor were these the only consequences of the break with Calhoun. Jackson and his closest friends were by this time bent on making Van Buren, instead of Calhoun, President after Jackson, but were doubtful of their ability to accomplish it at the next election. The President was therefore persuaded to run again. The Democrats in the legislature of Pennsylvania, acting on a hint from Lewis, sent him an address urging him to stand. If for a time he hesitated, he ceased to hesitate when it became apparent that Clay was going to be the candidate of the National Republicans. Clay, yielding to the appeals of his party friends, reappeared in the Senate at the opening of Congress in December, 1831, and now the duel between the two great party leaders grew fiercer than ever.

Clay returned to the Senate to find his tariff policy attacked by the nullifiers, his internal improvements policy blocked by the President's vetoes, and still a third policy which he and his party firmly supported vigorously attacked by the terrible man in the White House. The National Bank was in danger. Its charter expired in 1836, and the President in both his annual messages had gravely questioned the wisdom of granting another. He questioned the constitutionality of setting up such an institution, and he questioned the value and safety of the Bank as it existed. December 12, 1831, the National Republicans, assembled in their first national convention at Baltimore, nominated Clay for President, and called on the people to defeat Andrew Jackson in order to save the Bank. Jackson dauntlessly accepted the issue and gave the country to understand that either he or the Bank must go to the wall. For the time, even Calhoun and the nullifiers yielded the first place among his enemies to Clay, Biddle, and the Bank.

Biddle was president of the Bank, a handsome, accomplished man, a graceful writer, and a clever, though not always a safe financier. His ready pen first brought him into disfavor. Isaac Hill and Levi Woodbury, the Democratic Senators from New Hampshire, made complaints of Jeremiah Mason, an old Federalist, who was president of the Branch Bank at Portsmouth. Their charges were various, but they and others gave Jackson the idea that the Branch Bank in New Hampshire had used its power to oppose his friends and to help the Adams men. Biddle was called on to investigate. He did so, and defended Mason against all the charges. A long correspondence ensued, and Biddle went from Philadelphia, where the head Bank was, and made a visit to Portsmouth. His letters to the Secretary of the Treasury were courteous, well written, but also defiant. It was the Jackson men, he said, who were trying to draw the Bank into politics, and the Bank had constantly refused to go into politics in any way. He made out a very good case indeed, but the longer the correspondence lasted the stronger grew Jackson's conviction that the Bank was in politics, that it was fighting him, that it was corrupt, that it was dangerous to the liberties of the plain people who had sent him to the White House. Congress took up the matter, and committees of both Houses reported in favor of the Bank. The Supreme Court had already decided that the act establishing it was constitutional.

Clay boldly determined to force the fighting both on the tariff and on the Bank. The great measures of the Congress of 1831-2 were a new tariff law and a new Bank charter. The public debt was now nearly extinguished, and it was clearly advisable to reduce the revenue; but Clay and his followers made the reductions almost entirely on articles not produced in America, and so, in defiance of the nullifiers, made the new tariff as protective as the old. Jackson had gradually given up most of his protection ideas, and so the tariff did not please him. Clay, in fact, declared that for his "American system," as he called it, "he would defy the South, the President, and the Devil." Jackson was further defied by the Senate when it refused to confirm the nomination of Van Buren to be minister to Great Britain. The struggle raged through the whole session. Benton sturdily defended the President; Clay, Webster, and Calhoun were all, in one way or another, against him. It was a great session for the orators, and so far as Congress was concerned Clay had his way. But Lewis and Kendall were not idle; they were working not on Congress but on the people. In May, the Democrats nominated Jackson for President and Van Buren for Vice-President. In July, Congress finished its work with the Bank charter, and Jackson promptly answered with a veto, and so the two parties went to the country.

Jackson went into the campaign with an advantage drawn from his successful conduct of two foreign negotiations. His administration had secured from England an agreement by which the trade with the West Indies, closed to Americans ever since the Revolution, was opened again, and from France a promise to pay large claims for spoliations on American commerce which had been presented many times before. He was also undoubtedly supported by the great majority of the people in the stand he took against the nullifiers. What the people would decide about the tariff was doubtful; but as between a system, even though it were called the American system, and an old hero, the Democrats were not afraid of the people's choice. The great fight was over the Bank, and on that question Jackson was supported by the prejudices of the poor, who thought of the Bank merely as a rich men's institution, by the fears of the ignorant, who believed the Bank to be a mysterious and monstrous affair, and by the instinct of liberty in many others, who, though they did not believe the charges against Biddle, did feel that there was danger in so powerful a financial agency so closely connected with the government.

Moreover, the opposition was divided. A party bitterly opposed to Free Masonry had sprung into existence, and Jackson was a Mason. But the Anti-Masons, instead of supporting Clay, nominated a third candidate. South Carolina threw her votes away on a fourth.

Jackson got 219 electoral votes to 49 for Clay, 11 for Floyd, the nullification candidate, and seven for Wirt, the Anti-Mason candidate. His popular vote was more than twice Clay's, and he actually carried the New England States of Maine and New Hampshire. If, during his first term, he exercised his great office like a general, he entered upon the second with even a firmer belief that he ought to have his way in all things. The people had given an answer to Clay and Biddle and Calhoun and Marshall; to the corrupters of the government and the enemies of the President; to the nullifiers of the law and the slanderers of Peggy Eaton. He understood his overwhelming victory as the people's warrant to go on with all he had begun.

But neither the nullifiers nor the Bank were willing to give up. In November, 1832, a South Carolina convention passed an ordinance, to go into effect February 1, 1833, nullifying the tariff law, and took measures to defend its action by force. Jackson promptly sent Winfield Scott to South Carolina to make ready for fighting, employed a confidential agent to organize the Union men in the State, and called on Edward Livingston to help him with an address to his misguided countrymen. The pen of Livingston and the spirit of Jackson, working together, made the Nullification Proclamation a great state paper. It was a high-minded appeal to the second thought and the better nature of the Carolinians; an able statement of the national character of the government; a firm defiance to all enemies of the Union. It was the most popular act of the administration, and brought to its support men who had never supported it before. Benton and Webster joined hands; even Clay, who, like Jackson, loved his country with his whole heart, supported the President. Calhoun, alone of all his famous contemporaries, stood out against him. He left the Vice-President's seat, came down upon the floor as a Senator, and defended nullification against all the famous orators who crowded to assail it.

The President called on Congress to provide the means to enforce the law, and a so-called force bill was introduced. The Carolinians were defiant, and the country seemed on the verge of civil war; but Clay, by the second of his famous compromises, avoided the struggle. A new tariff law, providing for a gradual reduction of duties, was passed along with the force bill. The Carolinians chose the olive branch instead of the sword. The nullifiers first postponed and then repealed their ordinance.

Jackson was a national hero as he had never been before. In the summer of 1833, he made a journey to the Northeast, and even New England made him welcome. Harvard College made him a Doctor of Laws. As he rode through the streets of Boston, a merchant of Federalist traditions, who had closed his windows to show his principles, peeped through, and Jackson's bearing so touched him that he sent a child to wave the old gentleman a handkerchief. Andy of the Waxhaws was at the summit of his career. No other American could rival him in popularity; no other American had ever had such power over his countrymen since Washington frowned at the whisper that he might be a king.

But the great man was only a man, after all. He was in wretched health throughout his first term, and at times it did not seem that he could possibly live through it. His old wounds troubled him, and one day he laid bare his shoulder, gripped his cane with his free hand, and a surgeon cut out the ball from Jesse Benton's pistol. He was too ill to finish his New England tour, and hastened back to Washington.

But his opponents had little reason to rejoice in his illness. The summer was not spent before he had made up his mind to do the most daring act of his public life. He had vetoed the Bank's new charter, but the Bank itself was not destroyed. The public funds were still in its keeping; its power in the business world was as great as ever. He believed, moreover, that Biddle was using money freely to fight him, and would sooner or later get what he wanted from Congress. He prepared, therefore, to crush the Bank by withdrawing the deposits of public money and giving them into the keeping of other banks throughout the country. Blair, in "The Globe," set to work to convince the people that the Bank was not sound, and that the public funds were unsafe. Kendall was sent about the country to examine other banks. Congress voted against removing the deposits, but the old charter authorized the Secretary of the Treasury to do it, and the Secretary of the Treasury was now William Duane, of Philadelphia, a son of Jackson's early friend. There had been some changes in the cabinet after the second inauguration, Livingston had been appointed minister to France, the Secretary of the Treasury transferred to the State Department, and Duane called to the Treasury.

But Duane would not fall in with the President's plan. He did not believe the deposits were in danger, and refused to sign an order for removal. Jackson argued, then grew angry, and finally dismissed him. Duane defended his course ably. Lewis also advised against removal. Benton favored it, but in this he was almost alone among the leading public men. Jackson, however, was started, and he could not be stopped. Roger B. Taney, of Maryland, the Attorney-General, was made Secretary of the Treasury, and on September 26, 1833, three days after Duane's dismissal, the order was signed and a series of changes began that did not end until the whole financial system of the country was changed.

When Congress met, it proved to be, everything considered, probably the ablest legislature ever assembled in America. There were brilliant men of a new generation in the lower House, and Adams also was there. In the Senate, the great three were still supreme, and were now united against the President. The debates were long and furious. A panic throughout the country added to the excitement. Clay led the attack, Calhoun and Webster supported it; Benton bore the brunt of it. In the House, the Jackson men had a majority; in the Senate, the opposition. The Senate refused to confirm the nomination of Taney to be Secretary of the Treasury, and voted that the President had taken upon himself powers not given by the Constitution. The President sent in a fiery remonstrance, and the Senate voted not to receive it. Benton at once moved that the resolution of censure be expunged from the record, and declared he would keep that motion before the Senate until the people, by choosing a Jackson majority of Senators, should force it through.

The session closed with nothing done for the Bank, and nothing ever was done for it. When its charter expired in 1836, it got another from Pennsylvania, and kept going for some years. But Jackson had given it a deathblow. It fell into dangerous financial practices, failed, started again, failed a second time, staggered to its feet once more, and then went down in utter ruin and disgrace.

Its ruin was not accomplished without great disturbance to financial conditions. The country had been prosperous a long time. Money had been plentiful. Speculation had been the order of the day. The "pet banks," chosen to be the depositories of the government money, were badly managed. The surplus, distributed among the States, strengthened the impulse to wild speculation. Paper money was too plentiful. A dangerous financial condition prevailed, into whose causes and consequences we cannot here inquire. That and many other aspects of Jackson's administration can be satisfactorily treated only at considerable length. Jackson himself attributed all the trouble to Biddle and Clay; Biddle, he declared, was trying to ruin the country for revenge. The President even suspected Clay of setting on an insane person who attempted his life. He took no measures of a nature to restore health to business until near the end of his term. Then, acting as usual on his own responsibility, he issued a circular commonly called the "Specie Circular," requiring payments for public lands, which had formerly been made in bank paper, to be made in coin. That was like the thunderclap which precedes the storm: but the storm broke on his successor, not on him.

For a time it seemed as if he might also bequeath to his successor a foreign war. France had agreed to pay the spoliation claims, but the French Chambers failed to appropriate the money. Louis Philippe, the king, suggested to Livingston, the American Minister, that a stronger tone from the United States might stir the Chambers to action. Jackson was the last man in the world to hurt a cause by taking too mild a tone. In his message of 1834 to Congress, he took a tone so strong that it made the French Chambers too angry to pay. Thereupon, he suggested reprisals. The House, led by Adams, who never fell behind Jackson on a question of foreign relations, sustained the President. The Senate took no action. The French Chambers finally passed an appropriation, but with a proviso that no money should be paid until satisfactory explanations of the President's message were received. Jackson had no notion of apologizing, and feeling was rising in both countries. Diplomatic relations were broken off, and war was apparently very close, when, in the winter of 1835-6, England offered to mediate. An expression in Jackson's message of 1835, not meant as an apology, was somehow construed as such by the French ministry, and France agreed to pay.

The final settlement came at the very end of Jackson's administration. The presidential election of 1836 had fulfilled his wish that Van Buren should be his successor. In January, 1837, the resolution of censure was solemnly expunged from the records of the Senate. That body being now controlled by his friends, and his enemy, John Marshall, being dead, he named Taney Chief Justice, and the nomination was confirmed. He issued a farewell address to the people, after the manner of Washington, and stood, a white-haired, impressive figure, to watch the inauguration of Van Buren; then he journeyed home to The Hermitage to receive his last glorious welcome from his neighbors.

It was the most triumphant home-coming of them all. He had beaten all his enemies. Clay, wearied out with politics, was again in retirement; Adams, whom he found a President, was leading a minority of representatives in a new sectional struggle, the fight against slavery; Calhoun, whom he found but one step from the presidency, was a gloomy and tragical figure, the Ishmael of American politics. As for his friends, he left them in power everywhere,--in congress, on the bench, in the White House. To friends and enemies he had been like fate.

There was left for him a peaceful old age, and a calm and happy deathbed. Neighbors, political associates, old comrades, famous foreigners, visited The Hermitage to see the man who had played so great a part in history. Like Jefferson at Monticello, he guided with his counsel the party he had led. The long struggle over slavery was now begun, and soon the annexation of Texas took the first place among public questions. The old man had encouraged Houston to go to Texas, and had done all he could, and more than any other President would have dared, to forward the movement for independence. Now that Texas was ready to come into the Union, he heartily favored annexation. In 1844, Clay and Polk were candidates for the presidency, and Jackson's influence, still a power, was freely exerted for Polk and annexation. It was as if Clay, now an old man also, were once more about to lift the cup to his lips, and the relentless hand of Andrew Jackson dashed it to the ground.

Yet Andrew Jackson declared before he died that he forgave all his enemies. He had promised his wife, whose picture he wore in a great locket next his heart, whose Bible he read every day at the White House, that when he should be free of politics he would join himself to the church; if, he said, he made a profession while he was still before the people, his enemies would accuse him of hypocrisy. He kept his word. Trembling and weeping, he stood before the altar in the tiny church he had built for her and took the vows of a Christian. It had been hard for him to say that he forgave his enemies; hardest of all, to say that he forgave those who had attacked him while he was serving his country in the field. But after a long pause he told the minister he thought he could forgive even them.

June 8, 1845, in his seventy-ninth year, he died. His last words to those about him bade them meet him in heaven.

* * * * *

What is the rightful place in history of the fiery horseman in front of the White House? The reader must answer for himself when he has studied for himself all the great questions Jackson dealt with. Such a study will surely show that he made many mistakes, did much injustice to men, espoused many causes without waiting to hear the other side, was often bitter, violent, even cruel. It will show how ignorant he was on many subjects, how prejudiced on others. It will show him in contact with men who surpassed him in wisdom, in knowledge, in fairness of mind. It will deny him a place among those calm, just great men who can see both sides and yet strive ardently for the right side.

But the longest inquiry will not discover another American of his times who had in such ample measure the gifts of courage and will. Many had fewer faults, many superior talents, but none so great a spirit. He was the man who had his way. He was the American whose simple virtues his countrymen most clearly understood, whose trespasses they most readily forgave; and until Americans are altogether changed, many, like the Democrats of the 'Twenties and 'Thirties, will still "vote for Jackson,"--for the poor boy who fought his way, step by step, to the highest station; for the soldier who always went to meet the enemy at the gate; for the President who never shirked a responsibility; for the man who would not think evil of a woman or speak harshly to a child. Education, and training in statecraft, would have saved him many errors; culture might have softened the fierceness of his nature. But untrained, uncultivated, imperfect as he was, not one of his great contemporaries had so good a right to stand for American character.

Made in the USA
Middletown, DE
29 January 2018